EVERYTHING YOU NEED TO KNOW ABOUT
TAYLOR SWIFT

WELCOME

Taylor Swift signed her first record deal when she was just 14. Since then she has revolutionised the music industry, sold millions of albums worldwide breaking multiple records and amassed an army of fans. If you're a Swiftie, this is the perfect book for you. Inside you'll find everything you need to know about the superstar from where her journey started to her meteoric rise to fame, her life and relationships, challenges and triumphs. Discover what makes her a fashion guru, inspiration and icon whose name will go down in history.

FUTURE

EVERYTHING YOU NEED TO KNOW ABOUT
TAYLOR SWIFT

Future PLC Quay House, The Ambury, Bath, BA1 1UA

Editorial
Editor **Zara Gaspar**
Designer **Perry Wardell-Wicks**
Senior Art Editor **Andy Downes**
Head of Art & Design **Greg Whitaker**
Editorial Director **Jon White**

Contributors
Rebecca Bradbury; Jo Cole

Cover images
Getty images

Photography
All copyrights and trademarks are recognised and respected

Advertising
Media packs are available on request
Commercial Director **Clare Dove**

International
Head of Print Licensing **Rachel Shaw**
licensing@futurenet.com
www.futurecontenthub.com

Circulation
Head of Newstrade **Tim Mathers**

Production
Head of Production **Mark Constance**
Production Project Manager **Matthew Eglinton**
Advertising Production Manager **Joanne Crosby**
Digital Editions Controller **Jason Hudson**
Production Managers **Keely Miller, Nola Cokely, Vivienne Calvert, Fran Twentyman**

Printed in the UK

Distributed by Marketforce, 5 Churchill Place, Canary Wharf, London, E14 5HU
www.marketforce.co.uk – For enquiries, please email: mfcommunications@futurenet.com

EYNTKA Taylor Swift First Edition (MUB5310)
© 2023 Future Publishing Limited

We are committed to only using magazine paper which is derived from responsibly managed, certified forestry and chlorine-free manufacture. The paper in this bookazine was sourced and produced from sustainable managed forests, conforming to strict environmental and socioeconomic standards.

All contents © 2023 Future Publishing Limited or published under licence. All rights reserved. No part of this magazine may be used, stored, transmitted or reproduced in any way without the prior written permission of the publisher. Future Publishing Limited (company number 2008885) is registered in England and Wales. Registered office: Quay House, The Ambury, Bath BA1 1UA. All information contained in this publication is for information only and is, as far as we are aware, correct at the time of going to press. Future cannot accept any responsibility for errors or inaccuracies in such information. You are advised to contact manufacturers and retailers directly with regard to the price of products/services referred to in this publication. Apps and websites mentioned in this publication are not under our control. We are not responsible for their contents or any other changes or updates to them. This magazine is fully independent and not affiliated in any way with the companies mentioned herein.

FUTURE Connectors. Creators. Experience Makers.

Future plc is a public company quoted on the London Stock Exchange (symbol: FUTR)
www.futureplc.com

Chief Executive Officer **Jon Steinberg**
Non-Executive Chairman **Richard Huntingford**
Chief Financial and Strategy Officer **Penny Ladkin-Brand**

Tel +44 (0)1225 442 244

Widely Recycled

ipso. For press freedom with responsibility

CONTENTS

08 TAYLOR SWIFT
From a Christmas tree farm to the global stage, discover how it all started

20 FEARLESS
Whether it's speaking her truth in song lyrics or standing up to industry powerhouses, there is no superstar as courageous as Taylor Swift

40 LOVER
From faded romances to a fandom unlike any other, discover the relationships that have shaped Taylor's life and music

60 REPUTATION
How Taylor Swift went from country starlet to global superstar

80 FOLKLORE
Breaking records at every turn, Taylor's meteoric cultural impact will long do down in history

96 EVERMORE
Fashion icon, filmmaker and force for good, Taylor will be remembered for more than just her music

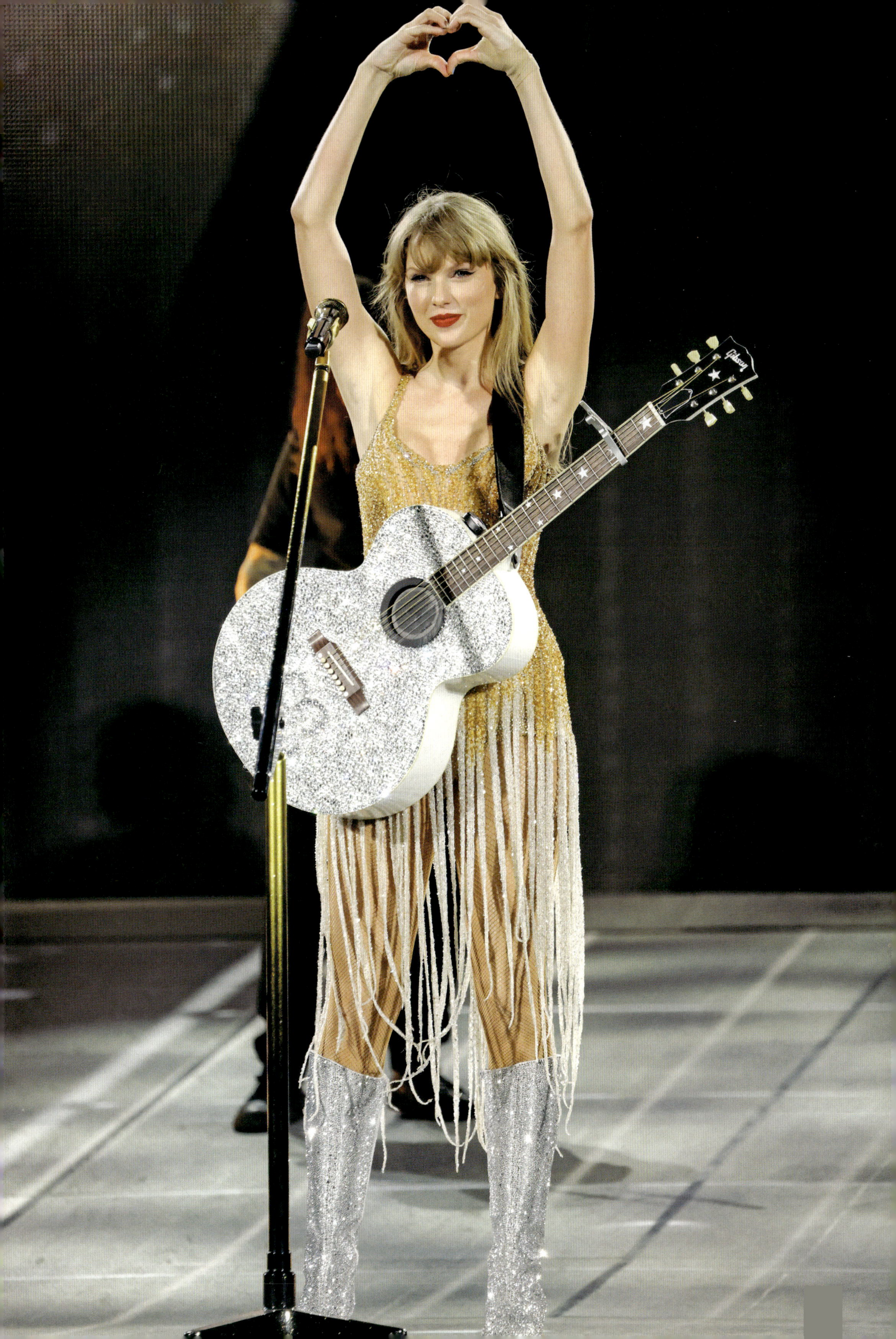
Gibson

TAYLOR SWIFT

TAYLOR SWIFT

FROM A CHRISTMAS TREE FARM TO THE GLOBAL STAGE, DISCOVER HOW IT ALL STARTED

TAYLOR SWIFT

TAYLOR SWIFT

TAYLOR SWIFT

Taylor Alison Swift was born on 13 December 1989 in West Reading, Pennsylvania. Some may say that Taylor's parents manifested their daughter's career path by naming her after the legendary singer-songwriter James Taylor, but music was already in her blood. Taylor was inspired to sing by her maternal grandmother, who was a professional opera singer. Recognise the name Marjorie from Taylor's *evermore* album? This track is Taylor's tribute to her late grandma.

Image: Michael Buckner / Getty images

SOME MAY SAY THAT TAYLOR'S PARENTS MANIFESTED THEIR DAUGHTER'S CAREER PATH BY NAMING HER AFTER JAMES TAYLOR, BUT MUSIC WAS ALREADY IN THE BLOOD

▶ After spending her early childhood on an 11-acre farm in Reading, Pennsylvania, Taylor moved with her mum, dad and brother to Wyomissing, where they rented this five-bedroom property on Grandview Boulevard. At 11 years old, Taylor joined the local junior high, but has since spoken about how hard she found it to fit in at school during this period of her life.

Image: MediaNews Group / Getty images

ONE OF THE MOST BEAUTIFUL THEMES TAYLOR EXPLORES IN HER SONGWRITING IS HER RELATIONSHIP WITH HER MUM

◀ One of the most beautiful themes Taylor explores in her songwriting is the relationship she shares with her mum, Andrea Swift. A former marketing manager, Andrea has always stood by her daughter and remains part of her close team. In *Miss Americana*, Taylor's 2020 Netflix documentary, the singer describes Andrea as her 'favourite person in the world'.

Image: Denise Truscello / Getty images

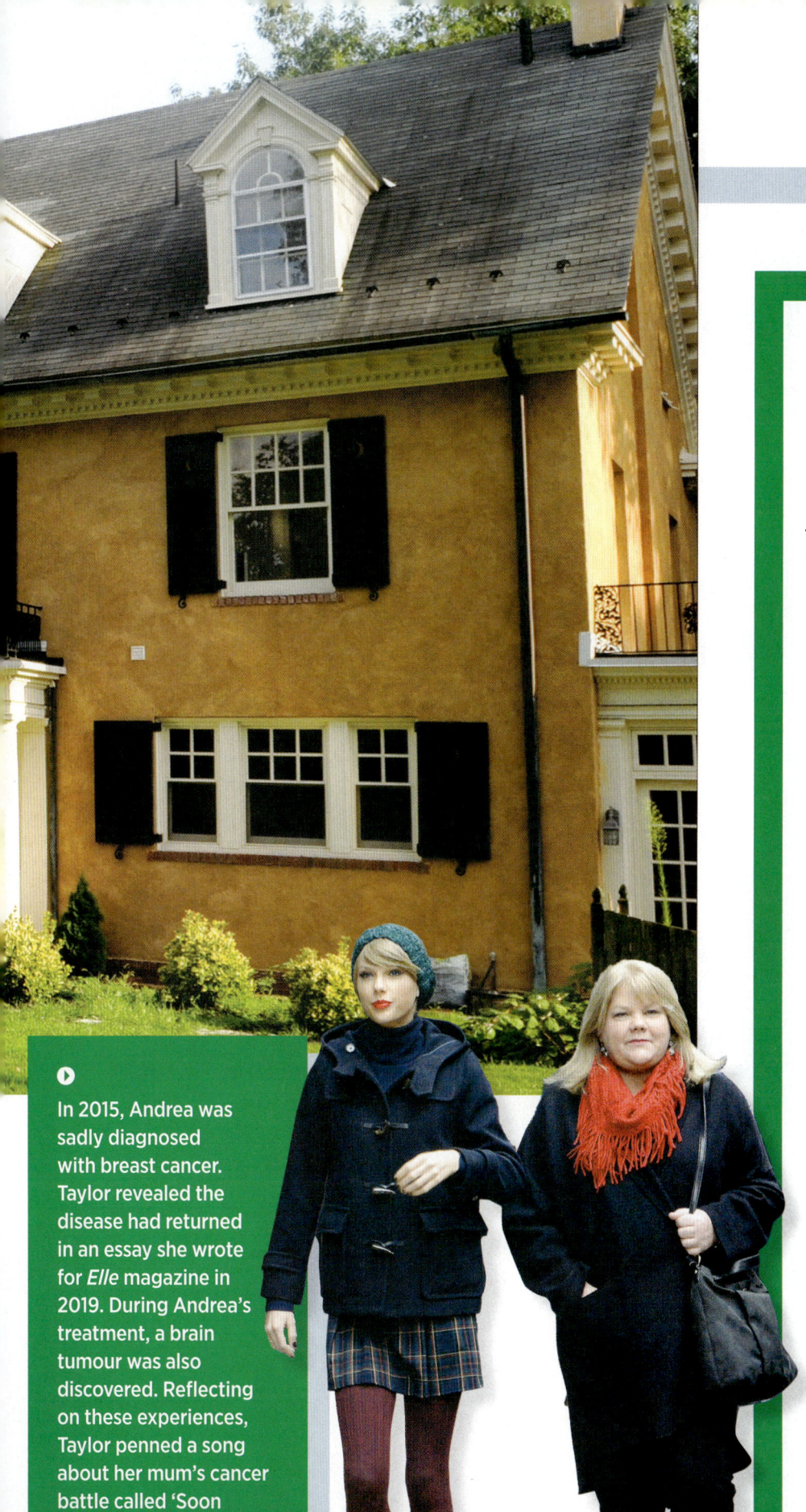

TAYLOR SWIFT

Did you know?

THE FIRST SONG TAYLOR LEARNT TO PLAY ON THE GUITAR WAS 'KISS ME' BY SIXPENCE NONE THE RICHER. BETTER KNOWN FOR THEIR ALTERNATIVE ROCK SOUND, THE BAND PROVIDED A SLIGHTLY DIFFERENT SORT OF INSPIRATION FOR TAYLOR, WHO CITES HER ROLE MODELS AS THE COUNTRY MUSIC ARTISTS LEANN RHIMES, SHANIA TWAIN AND THE DIXIE CHICKS. IT WAS AFTER WATCHING A DOCUMENTARY ABOUT FAITH HILL THAT TAYLOR BECAME SURE SHE NEEDED TO MOVE TO NASHVILLE TO PURSUE HER DREAMS. SHE ALSO HAD THE FORESIGHT FROM A VERY YOUNG AGE TO KNOW SHE NEEDED TO OFFER THE INDUSTRY SOMETHING DIFFERENT, WHICH IS WHY SHE PICKED UP THE GUITAR AND STARTED WRITING HER OWN MUSIC.

▶ In 2015, Andrea was sadly diagnosed with breast cancer. Taylor revealed the disease had returned in an essay she wrote for *Elle* magazine in 2019. During Andrea's treatment, a brain tumour was also discovered. Reflecting on these experiences, Taylor penned a song about her mum's cancer battle called 'Soon You'll Get Better', which featured on her 2019 album, *Lover*.

Image: Rick Kern / Getty images

TAYLOR SWIFT

INSTEAD OF GIVING AN INTERVIEW SHE CONTRIBUTED A POEM

🔽 Taylor is also close to her dad, Scott Kingsley Swift, a former stockbroker who the singer describes as 'a big teddy bear who tells me everything I do is perfect'. In 2004, when Taylor was just 14 years old, he transferred to his firm's Nashville office and relocated to the city with his family so Taylor could be closer to the song-writing opportunities the Tennessee capital offered.

Image: Charley Gallay / Stringer / Getty images

🔼 But Taylor began dedicating songs to her family far earlier than this. Back in 2008, the singer included the song 'The Best Day' on her second album, *Fearless*. The lyrics pay tribute to her mum, dad and brother (picture above), and recall childhood memories of pumpkin patches and tractor rides.

Image: Gardiner Anderson/Bauer-Griffin / Getty images

TAYLOR SWIFT

Fun Fact

TAYLOR DOESN'T SOLELY USE HER UNRIVALLED WRITING SKILLS FOR CRAFTING LYRICS AND SIGNING AUTOGRAPHS. WHEN THE STAR WAS IN 4TH GRADE, SHE WON A NATIONAL POETRY CONTEST WITH A POEM CALLED 'MONSTER IN MY CLOSET'. WE CAN ONLY ASSUME THE STAR HAS CONTINUED TO PEN POETRY ALONGSIDE WRITING SONGS, AS IN 2017 SHE APPEARED ON THE COVER OF BRITISH *VOGUE*, BUT INSTEAD OF GIVING AN INTERVIEW SHE CONTRIBUTED HER OWN POEM CALLED 'THE TRICK TO HOLDING ON'. SHE'S ALSO OPENED UP ABOUT WRITING AN UNPUBLISHED NOVEL WHEN SHE WAS JUST 14 YEARS OLD CALLED *A GIRL CALLED GIRL*.

Image: Kevin Mazur / Getty Images

TAYLOR SWIFT

▶ When Taylor first arrived on the music scene she was rarely seen without a pair of cowboy boots. The footwear of choice for many country stars, they signify the singer's musical roots. Not only did she grow up listening to the genre, but she also began crafting her own country songs as a young teen. For two hours after school every Tuesday she would have writing sessions with the lyricist Liz Rose, who would become one of Taylor's long-term writing partners.

Image: Rusty Russell / Getty images

△ Taylor's headshot now adorns a wall inside the iconic Bluebird Cafe alongside signed photographs of other country songwriters who have also performed at the in-the-round venue. The success of her first few albums catapulted country into mainstream and introduced a new audience of younger fans to the genre.

Image: Robert Alexander / Getty images

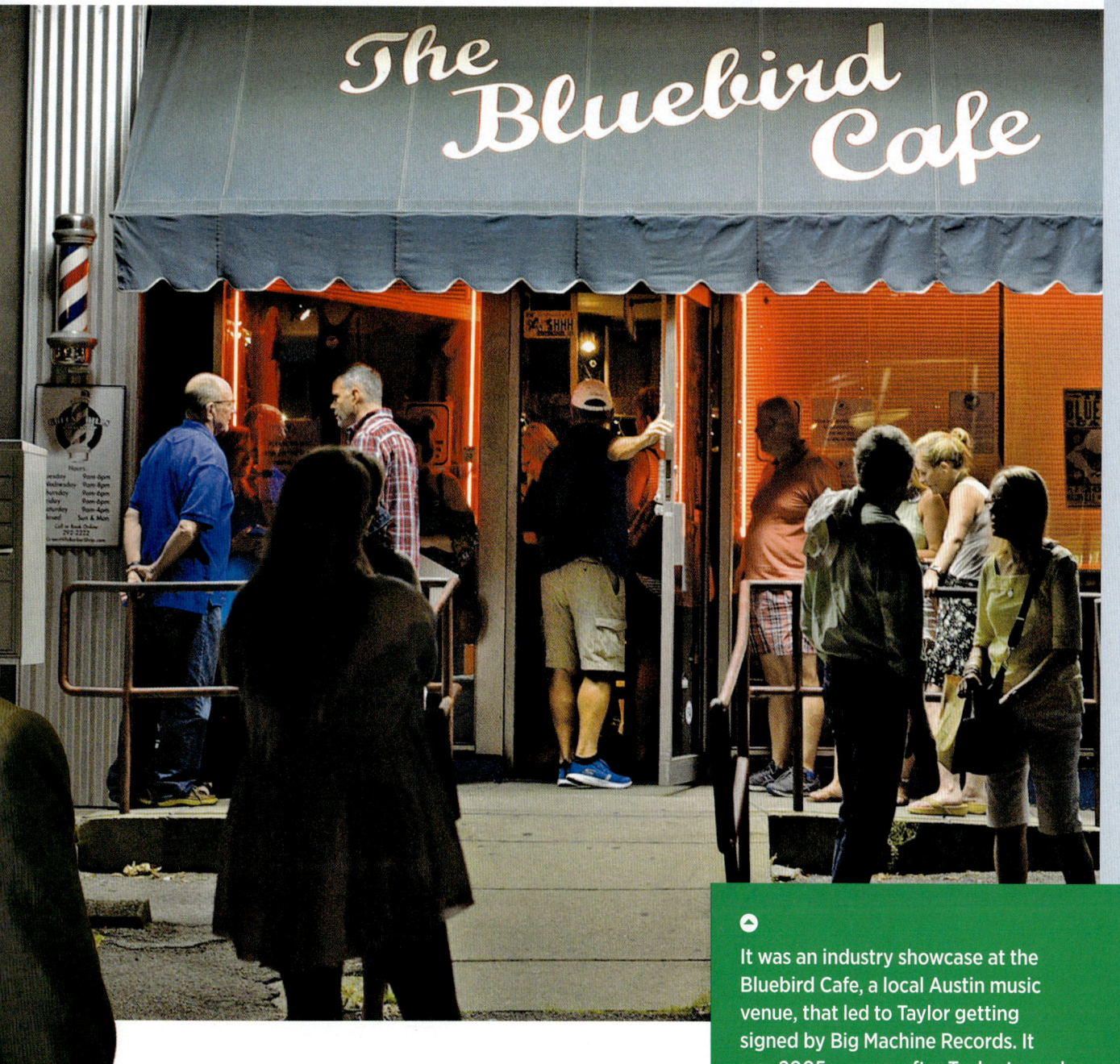

TAYLOR SWIFT

Austin Kingsley Swift is Taylor's only sibling. Three years younger than his sister, he reportedly has fond memories of childhood holidays spent in their parent's Jersey beach house together. After a stint of studying photography in college, he switched to acting and graduated from the University of Notre Dame in Indiana in 2015. Since then he's had roles in sitcoms and films, including *Braking for Whales* and *We Summon the Darkness*.

Image: Rick Diamond / Getty images

It was an industry showcase at the Bluebird Cafe, a local Austin music venue, that led to Taylor getting signed by Big Machine Records. It was 2005 – a year after Taylor turned down a development deal with Sony/ATV as she felt the firm didn't value her song-writing abilities. Big Machine Records, on the other hand, was a new, independent record label set up by Scott Borchetta, which would offer Taylor more control over her musical direction.

Image: Robert Alexander / Getty images

Did you know?

IF TAYLOR LIKES ANYTHING MORE THAN MAKING MUSIC, IT'S HER THREE GORGEOUS PEDIGREE CATS. THE ELDEST IS A TABBY SCOTTISH FOLD CALLED MEREDITH GREY, NAMED AFTER THE PROTAGONIST IN TV SHOW *GREY'S ANATOMY*. NEXT UP IS ANOTHER SCOTTISH FOLD CALLED OLIVA BENSON, NAMED AFTER THE LEAD CHARACTER IN *LAW AND ORDER: SVU*. OLIVIA HAS EVEN FEATURED IN ONE OF TAYLOR'S DIET COKE COMMERCIALS, AS WELL AS HER VIDEO FOR 'BLANK SPACE'. THE YOUNGEST CAT IS A BLUE-EYED RAGDOLL NAMED BENJAMIN BUTTON, WHICH TAYLOR ADOPTED AFTER HE FEATURED IN HER MUSIC VIDEO FOR 2019'S 'ME!' WITH PANIC! AT THE DISCO'S BRENDON URIE.

Image: Kevin Mazur / Getty Images

- Taylor began taking guitar lessons with local computer repairman and part-time musician Ronnie Cremer when she was around 12 years old. He would come to Taylor's house twice a week to teach her chords and help her write songs. The singer is now also a master of the banjo, ukulele and piano, as seen in many of her live performances.

Image: Mark Humphrey / Getty images

- The first single Taylor released was 'Tim McGraw', a song about a summer romance coming to an end, which references the country artist in the chorus. The idea came to Taylor while in maths class and she finessed the song after school with Liz Rose. Taylor has since performed with Tim and opened for him in 2007, as part of his world tour with his wife, Faith Hill.

Image: Frederick Breedon IV / Getty images

TAYLOR SWIFT

● Taylor is seen here with her brother attending an American football game in 2010, a decade or so after making some of her first performances at sports events. Her first major gig was at just 11 years old, when she sang the US national anthem at a Philadelphia 76ers basketball game. And when it comes to NFL, Taylor's a big Philadelphia Eagles fan.

Image: Sipa US / Alamy Stock Photo

● Swifties will no doubt know that Taylor spent her early childhood growing up on a Christmas tree farm, with her love of the festive season reflected in her music. Here is Taylor in 2007, when she performed at the Rockefeller Tree Lighting Ceremony in New York City. She has also penned original Christmas songs, added holiday-inspired lyrics to songs such as 'Lover' and is even said to incorporate festive decorations into her birthday celebrations on 13th December every year.

Image: Kevin Mazur / Getty images

19

FEARLESS

FEARLESS

WHETHER IT'S SPEAKING HER TRUTH IN SONG LYRICS OR STANDING UP TO INDUSTRY POWERHOUSES, THERE IS NO SUPERSTAR AS COURAGEOUS AS TAYLOR SWIFT

FEARLESS

FEARLESS

Taylor knew she had to stand out amid the Nashville music scene in order to get a record deal, so she learnt to play the guitar and started writing her own songs. Her daring paid off, as she harnessed her natural song-writing abilities and discovered a way to express her thoughts and emotions. Here she is performing with her personalised guitar on her first tour in 2007.

Image: Jason Moore / Alamy images

Even as a teenager, Taylor proved she was fearless. At 13 years old, she had the courage to pitch herself to record labels. Pictured here in 2006, the year her debut album was released, she has since explained the source of her bravery: "It's because I could never feel the kind of rejection that I felt in middle school. Because in the music industry, if they're gonna say no to you, at least they're gonna be polite about it."

Image: John Shearer / WireImage

FEARLESS

Taylor opened her Fearless Tour dressed in this now-iconic marching band ensemble. Explaining the name choice for her second album, she said: "Fearless is getting back up and fighting for what you want over and over again... It's fearless to have faith that someday things will change." Such determination encapsulates her approach to both her career and life in general.

Image: Jason Kempin / Getty images

TAYLOR KNEW SHE HAD TO STAND OUT, SO SHE LEARNT TO PLAY THE GUITAR AND STARTED WRITING HER OWN SONGS. HER DARING PAID OFF

Performing her single 'Should Have Said No' at the Academy of Country Music Awards in 2008, Taylor began wearing a hoodie and jeans before changing on stage into this little black dress. The lyrics are based on a conversation she had when confronting her cheating ex-boyfriend. Taylor makes it clear she'll never get back with him, providing an empowering message for listeners to have the confidence to know their self-worth – a message she continues to push to this day.

Image: Ethan Miller / Alamy images

FEARLESS

● This was the moment Taylor's high-profile feud with rapper Kanye West began. It was the 2009 MTV VMAs and Taylor was up on stage collecting the Best Female Video Award for 'You Belong With Me'. But mid-speech, Kanye stormed the stage, grabbed the mic and declared Beyonce should have won. What followed was a masterclass from Taylor on how to graciously forgive, stand up to bullies and have the fortitude to prove naysayers wrong.

Image: Kevin Mazur / WireImage / Getty images

WHAT FOLLOWED WAS A MASTERCLASS FROM TAYLOR ON HOW TO GRACIOUSLY FORGIVE AND STAND UP TO BULLIES

Did you know?

TAYLOR HAS PROVEN HER STRENGTH WHEN STANDING UP TO INDUSTRY BIG WIGS, AND WHEN IT COMES TO BEING WRONGED BY HER BEST MATES, SHE WILL SIMILARLY DEFEND HERSELF. CASE IN POINT IS THE 2014 TRACK 'BAD BLOOD', A SONG ABOUT BEING BETRAYED BY A CLOSE FRIEND. MANY BELIEVE THE SONG'S SUBJECT IS KATY PERRY AFTER THE PAIR ALLEGEDLY FELL OUT OVER SOME BACKING DANCERS. ALTHOUGH TAYLOR HAS DENIED THIS, THE WELL-KNOWN FEUD CAME TO AN END IN MAY 2018 WHEN KATY SENT TAYLOR A LITERAL OLIVE BRANCH AHEAD OF THE OPENING NIGHT OF HER REPUTATION TOUR. IN RETURN, TAYLOR SENT KATY SOME COOKIES ADORNED WITH FROSTING THAT SPELT 'PEACE AT LAST'.

Image: Clive Davis / Getty Images

FEARLESS

Apologies can be a true sign of courage, which is something Taylor showcased in her track 'Back to December' from the album *Speak Now*. Performing the song here at the CMA Awards in 2010, the singer wrote the song as a remorseful plea to an ex-boyfriend. The entire album is about "figuring out how you feel and saying something about it".

Image: Rick Diamond / Getty images

FEARLESS

IN RESPONSE TO KANYE'S RUDE INTERRUPTION, TAYLOR PENNED A SONG CALLED 'INNOCENT' FOR HER THIRD ALBUM

▼ As this hug testifies, Taylor and Kanye had made peace by 2015. But it did not last long. He released a track the next year called 'Famous', which includes the lyrics: "I feel like me and Taylor might still have sex. Why? I made that b**** famous." The rapper then claimed Taylor gave the line her blessing – something the country star denied in a statement where she also called out his misogynistic language.

Image: Kevin Mazur / Getty images

▲ Taylor poses here in 2012 with singer Rita Ora and reality TV star Kim Kardashian – Kanye West's ex-wife who also had a role to play in the public fallout. After the release of 'Famous' in 2016, Kim published footage appearing to show Taylor giving her approval of the lyrics. Four years later, the clip was proven to be edited, but at the time Taylor received a barrage of online hate, which contributed to her taking a prolonged break from the public eye.

Image: Dave Hogan / MTV / Getty images

FEARLESS

▶ In response to Kanye's rude interruption, Taylor penned a song called 'Innocent' for her third album, Speak Now. The lyrics of the gentle pop ballad sympathise with a man who has committed wrongdoings, demonstrating Taylor's boldness to forgive. She debuted the track at the 2010 MTV Video Music Awards, as pictured here.

Image: Kevin Mazur / Getty images

▶ Not only did Taylor have to contend with the Kanye West controversy but she also had to deal with intense media scrutiny about her personal life. Retreating out of the limelight for a year, she made the ultimate comeback with 'Look What You Made Me Do' – the first single from her 2017 album, *reputation*, which bravely reclaims the narrative of her public perception. After its release, she went on to win four awards at the 2018 American Music Awards.

Image: Frazer Harrison / Getty images

FEARLESS

▼ Clad in a red sequined ringmaster costume, Taylor performs 'We Are Never Ever Getting Back Together' as part of her Red Tour. On the album *RED*, Taylor is unafraid to showcase all the messy emotions she's experienced in her love life, while the song '22' is Taylor flaunting her youth in the face of critics who previously dismissed her song-writing prowess because of her young age.

Image: Scott Barbour / TAS / Getty images

▼ Performing the single 'Blank Space' with a golf club in hand was one of the most memorable images from Taylor's 1989 World Tour. The track is another tongue-in-cheek, self-referential response to the media's obsession with her love life and its portrayal of her, in her own words, as "a girl who's crazy but seductive but glamorous but nuts but manipulative".

Image: Steve Granitz / WireImage / Getty images

Taylor racked up many awards for her 2014 single 'Shake It Off', taken from her fifth studio album, *1989*. Inspired by her detractors, especially the tabloids, the song is Taylor's proactive, satirical stance to take back control of her public image. The lines "I go on too many dates / But I can't make 'em stay / At least that's what people say" is a takedown of the news outlets that portrayed her as a serial dater.

Image: Kevin Winter / Getty images

INSPIRED BY HER DETRACTORS, ESPECIALLY THE TABLOIDS, THE SONG IS TAYLOR'S PROACTIVE, SATIRICAL STANCE

FEARLESS

While releasing multiple award-winning albums, Taylor was having to contend with a court case – which led to an office block opposite the courthouse in Denver making signs in support of the singer. It began in June 2013 when DJ David Mueller groped the singer while they were posing for a photo. After Taylor's team reported the incident to his employers, he was sacked from his job at KYGO radio station – a dismissal that caused him to file a lawsuit against Taylor for defamation.

Image: Joe Mahoney / Getty images

The handmade signs appeared when Taylor's counterclaim against Mueller went to court. The jury eventually ruled the DJ as guilty and Taylor was awarded a requested sum of $1. She also pledged to donate 'an unspecified amount' to organisations aimed at helping sexual assault victims. Going through such an ordeal under the public gaze is another sign of Taylor's fearlessness and strength, helping women find the courage to speak up against sexual harassment.

Image: Theo Stroomer / Getty images

Fun Fact

AFTER TAYLOR'S CIVIL CASE AGAINST MUELLER, SHE WAS NAMED ONE OF 'THE SILENCE BREAKERS' IN *TIME* MAGAZINE'S ANNUAL PERSON OF THE YEAR EDITION IN 2017. SHE SHARED THE FRONT COVER WITH FOUR OTHER WOMEN WHO WERE APPLAUDED FOR TELLING THEIR STORIES ABOUT SEXUAL ASSAULT AND HARASSMENT. THEY INCLUDE FORMER UBER EMPLOYEE SUSAN FOWLER WHO CALLED OUT SILICON VALLEY'S FRAT CULTURE AND ASHLEY JUDD, ONE OF THE FIRST WOMEN TO ACCUSE HARVEY WEINSTEIN OF SEXUAL HARASSMENT. YOU CAN ALSO SPOT A MYSTERY ARM IN THE BOTTOM RIGHT-HAND CORNER. THIS REPRESENTS THOSE WOMEN WHO ARE UNABLE TO SPEAK OUT DUE TO THE POTENTIALLY DIRE REPERCUSSIONS.

Image: Richard Levine / Alamy Images

▶ Taylor is snapped here at an awards ceremony in 2015 with Scott Borchetta, the founder of Big Machine Records – the label the singer signed a 13-year deal with in 2006. On the surface all was well, but friction developed in 2018 when Taylor's contract ended and she switched to Universal's Republic Records, spurring a high-profile dispute about music ownership and artists' rights.

Image: Kevin Mazur / WireImage/ Getty images

▼ Taylor high-fives her fans during the Tampa show of her Reputation Stadium Tour on 11 May 2018. The date marked the one-year anniversary of winning her civil case against Mueller, and she gave concert-goers an emotional speech reflecting on the trial and thanking her fans for their support throughout the ordeal. She also stressed the need for better justice for sexual assault victims.

Image: Kevin Mazur / Getty images

FEARLESS

> In an explosive Tumbler post, Taylor described Braun's buyout as her "worst case scenario", accusing him of "incessant, manipulative bullying" – after all, he had been working with Kanye West when the rapper slated her in his track 'Famous'. But Haim (pictured), Halsey and Iggy Azalea were among the musicians to publicly support Taylor over the controversy, applauding her willingness to speak out against industry figures as powerful as Braun in an effort to protect her work and artistry.
>
> Image: Matt Winkelmeyer / VF23 / Getty images

FEARLESS

Fun Fact

TAYLOR MADE A POWERFUL STATEMENT AT THE 2019 AMERICAN MUSIC AWARDS, WHEN SHE TOOK TO THE STAGE TO PERFORM A MEDLEY OF HER BIGGEST HITS. AT THE TIME OF THIS, BRAUN WAS SUPPOSEDLY BLOCKING HER FROM SINGING HER PAST TRACKS AT THE ANNUAL CEREMONY. HITTING BACK AT THE MUSIC MOGUL, SHE APPEARED ON THE STAGE WEARING AN OVERSIZED WHITE SHIRT, WITH THE NAMES OF HER FIRST FIVE ALBUMS EMBLAZONED ACROSS IT. A GROUP OF CHILDREN THEN JOINED TAYLOR ON STAGE, WEARING MATCHING ENSEMBLES THAT FANS SPECULATE IS AN IMPLICATION THAT FUTURE GENERATIONS SHOULD BE ABLE TO OWN THE WORK THEY CREATE.

Image: Emma McIntyre / Getty Images

◀ Months after Taylor's contract with Big Machine Records ended, the record label announced it had been acquired by music mega-manager Scooter Braun. Taylor had been trying to acquire her master recordings – the original recorded versions of her tracks – from Borchetta for years. But after refusing to budge, he had passed the ownership rights over to Braun, who would now profit every time a fan streamed or downloaded a Taylor Swift track. Borchetta and Braun are pictured here together.

Image: Kevin Mazur / Getty images

HITTING BACK AT THE MUSIC MOGUL, SHE APPEARED ON THE STAGE WEARING A WHITE SHIRT, WITH THE NAMES OF HER FIRST FIVE ALBUMS ON IT

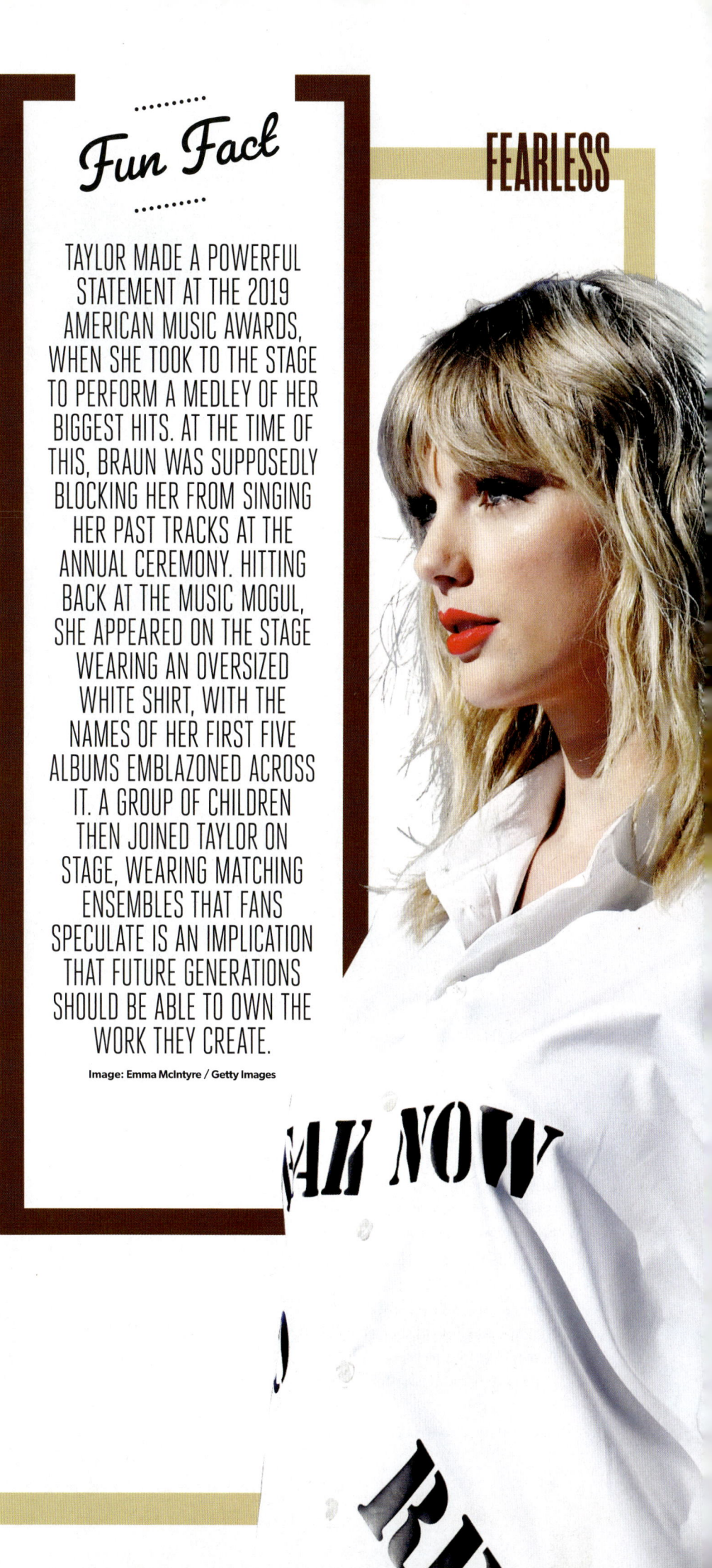

FEARLESS

● The master recordings controversy was not the first time Taylor made a stance about how the music industry operates. In 2014, the singer pulled her music from Spotify, arguing that artists receive a tiny royalty per song play. But she made a return to streaming services in 2017 to thank fans for her album, *1989*, passing ten million sales.

Image: Michelangelo Oprandi / Alamy images

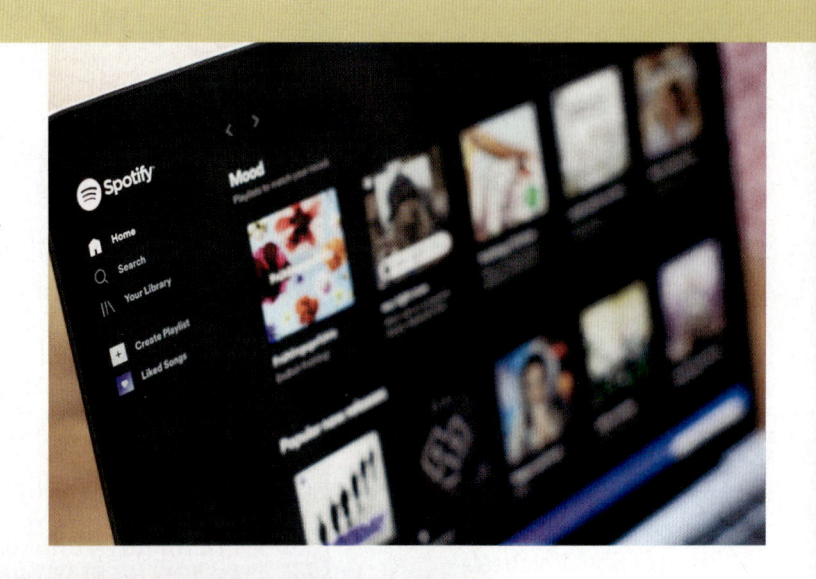

◐ Master recordings regularly change hands, but never hit the headlines, making Taylor's actions even more admirable. She also announced plans to re-record her first five albums, releasing *Fearless (Taylor's Version)* in April 2021 and *RED (Taylor's Version)* in November 2021. At the 2019 Billboard Women in Music Event, she addressed the 'toxic male privilege' of Braun in her acceptance speech for winning the inaugural Woman of the Decade award.

Image: Kevin Mazur / Getty images

● Opening the 2019 Billboard Music Awards with Brendon Urie, Taylor performs 'Me!', the lead single from *Lover* – her first album with new label Republic Records. All about embracing individuality, the song is Taylor's declaration that she has found success in the freedom to be herself – and encourages her fans to do the same.

Image: Ethan Miller / Getty images

FEARLESS

▶ Taylor has also spoken out in support of friend and fellow musician, Kesha. The 'Tik Tok' and 'Take It Off 'singer had her own high-profile legal battles to contend with involving her former producer, Dr Luke, who she alleges sexually assaulted her. Among other supporters such as Lady Gaga, Ariana Grande and Miley Cyrus, Taylor posted her support on social media and donated $250,000 to help Kesha with financial needs.

Image: Frazer Harrison /FilmMagic) / Getty images

● This rainbow-hued stage production is from Taylor's performance at the 2019 MTV VMAs. At the awards ceremony she won the 'Video of the Year' accolade for 'You Need to Calm Down', a gay anthem in which Taylor voices her support for the LGTBQ+ community. The release of the track resulted in a spike of donations to GLAAD, an organisation battling for LGTBQ+ acceptance, which Taylor namechecked in the lyrics.

Image: Mike Coppola / Getty images

35

FEARLESS

Did you know?

When Taylor revealed her long-running struggle to reclaim her musical catalogue, she also enabled other artists to question their rights. After watching Taylor's battle play out, singer-songwriter Olivia Rodrigo announced she had negotiated with her record label to own her masters. Canadian musician Bryan Adams was inspired by Taylor to re-record his own back catalogue after a disagreement with his record label. Joe Jonas, Rita Ora, Snoop Dogg and Ashanti are among the other artists who have admitted they would like to re-record their work or purchase their masters following Taylor's example.

Image: Lionel Hahn/ Getty Images

FEARLESS

▲ A fan holds up a banner at a Taylor Swift performance in London in 2012 referencing the US elections, despite the singer remaining famously mute on all things politics. But six years later, when Taylor publicly endorsed the Democratic candidate Phil Bredesen for the 2018 senate race, she caused a surge in people registering to vote, an effect the media called the 'Swift Lift'.

Image: Samir Hussein / Getty images

▶ On the opening night of her Eras Tour in Arizona, Taylor entered the stage wearing this bejewelled Versace bodysuit. The first song on the set list was 'Miss Americana and the Heartbreak Prince', a track that Taylor wrote to capture her disillusionment with the state of the American political climate in 2018. It represents one of the singer's first attempts to become more socially engaged.

Image: Kevin Mazur / Getty images

▲ Taylor performed 'The Man' during her one-off City of Lover concert in Paris on 9 September 2019 and the live track was released as a single. In the song, Taylor imagines how she would be treated as a man, calling out double standards, toxic masculinity and the objectification of women. It is an important portrayal of the sexist behaviour women face every day.

Image: Dave Hogan / Getty images

FEARLESS

◀ Taylor had a different political game plan for the 2020 US elections. In her Netflix documentary, *Miss Americana*, she expressed regret at not denouncing Donald Trump when he ran for office in 2016. But this time, she posted on Twitter that she would be voting for the Democratic presidential nominee, Joe Biden.

Image: Kevin Dietsch / Getty images

Voting isn't the only area where Taylor has become more vocal. In 2018, she donated to the March for Our Lives rally, a student-led movement against gun violence. Then after the death of George Floyd, who was wrongfully killed by a police officer in May 2020, she used her platform to speak out about the lack of police accountability and the institution's racist behaviour.

Image: David McNew / Getty images

Fun Fact

IF YOU'RE FAMILIAR WITH TAYLOR'S DISCOGRAPHY, YOU MIGHT NOTICE ON EVERY ALBUM THAT TRACK FIVE IS THE MOST HEART-WRENCHING. FROM 'COLD AS YOU' ON HER SELF-TITLED DEBUT TO 'YOU'RE ON YOUR OWN, KID' ON HER 2021 RELEASE *MIDNIGHTS*, THE TRADITION SHOWS TAYLOR IS UNAFRAID TO SHARE HER MOST EMOTIONAL INSIGHTS. "I DIDN'T REALISE I WAS DOING THIS, BUT AS I WAS MAKING ALBUMS, I GUESS I WAS JUST KIND OF PUTTING A VERY VULNERABLE, PERSONAL, HONEST, EMOTIONAL SONG AS TRACK FIVE," SHE ONCE EXPLAINED DURING AN INSTAGRAM LIVE. THE SINGER EVEN WON A GRAMMY AWARD FOR 'WHITE HORSE', WHICH IS TRACK NUMBER FIVE ON THE ALBUM *FEARLESS*.

Image: Robyn Beck / Getty Images

SHE USED HER PLATFORM TO SPEAK OUT ABOUT POLICE ACCOUNTABILITY

LOVER

LOVER

FROM FADED ROMANCES TO A FANDOM UNLIKE ANY OTHER, DISCOVER THE RELATIONSHIPS THAT HAVE SHAPED TAYLOR'S LIFE AND MUSIC

LOVER

Taylor's first high-profile relationship was with Joe Jonas in 2008. But the Jonas Brothers frontman and the 'Love Story' singer only dated for a few months before he broke up with her on a 27-second phone call. Seen here appearing with the band as a guest performer on their Burnin' Up Tour, Taylor was reportedly inspired to write the songs 'Last Kiss' and 'Forever and Always' after the relationship came to its brutal end.

Image: Everett Collection / Disney / Alamy images

When Taylor was 19 years old, she began dating a 31-year-old John Mayer after collaborating with him on his song 'Half of My Heart'. The romance lasted for about four months, but Taylor had enough material to pen the power ballad 'Dear John' – an obvious dig at the singer and how he pursued her despite her young age.

Image: Kevin Mazur / WireImage / Getty images

▶ Affectionately known as Taylor Squared, Taylor Swift and *Twilight* star Taylor Lautner began dating in 2009. The couple met when they co-starred as high school sweethearts in the romantic comedy *Valentine's Day*. Her song 'Back to December', with the lyrics 'Your tanned skin, your sweet smile', is allegedly about the actor and her regret for the way she ended things.

Image: Moviestore Collection / Alamy images

THE LACK OF PRIVACY AND AGE GAP WASN'T WORKING FOR JAKE, SO HE CALLED IT QUITS. LEGEND HAS IT HE STOOD TAYLOR UP ON HER 21ST BIRTHDAY PARTY

▶ Regularly papped together around New York City and Los Angeles, Taylor and actor Jake Gyllenhaal couldn't escape the spotlight when they dated in 2010. But apparently the lack of privacy and ten-year age gap wasn't working for Jake, so he called it quits. Legend has it he even stood Taylor up on her 21st birthday party, inspiring the singer to write a bunch of songs featured on her *RED* album, including 'We Are Never Getting Back Together', 'The Last Time' and 'All Too Well'.

Image: Gareth Cattermole / Getty images

43

LOVER

▸ Harry Styles and Taylor Swift were spotted catching up together at the 2023 Grammy Awards – ten years after a short-lived romance. Despite dating for only three or four months, the couple shared paper aeroplane necklaces, kissed in Times Square on New Year's Eve and even got into a snowmobile accident together. Fans speculate that 'I Knew You Were Trouble' and 'Out of the Woods' were written about the ex-One Direction band member.

Image: Frazer Harrison / Getty images

▲ Mutual friend and fellow singer-songwriter Ellie Goulding introduced Taylor to Scottish DJ Calvin Harris at the Elle Style Awards in 2015. The romance blossomed, with the couple sharing PDAs at music awards, red carpet appearances and adorable Instagram posts. But not long after celebrating their one-year anniversary, the relationship ended abruptly. Some sources say the couple simply weren't compatible, while others claim he was intimidated by her success.

Image: Kevin Winter / Getty images

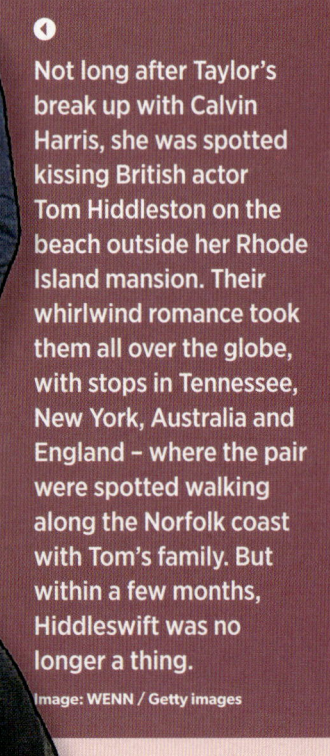

◂ Not long after Taylor's break up with Calvin Harris, she was spotted kissing British actor Tom Hiddleston on the beach outside her Rhode Island mansion. Their whirlwind romance took them all over the globe, with stops in Tennessee, New York, Australia and England – where the pair were spotted walking along the Norfolk coast with Tom's family. But within a few months, Hiddleswift was no longer a thing.

Image: WENN / Getty images

LOVER

Did you know?

Top of every Swiftie's wish list is to be invited to one of Taylor's Secret Sessions. These fan-only parties began in 2014, when Taylor requested the company of some of her closest allies so she could play them her album prior to its release. Since then, the get-togethers have taken place in her various homes, from New York and Nashville to Los Angeles, Rhode Island and London. But how does Taylor pick her guests? Apparently, the singer indulges in what she calls #TAYLURKING – tracking her own fans on social media to compile the next guest list. But what happens in a secret session, stays in a secret session.

Image: Mark Metcalfe / Getty Images

APPARENTLY, THE SINGER INDULGES IN #TAYLURKING – TRACKING HER OWN FANS ON SOCIAL MEDIA

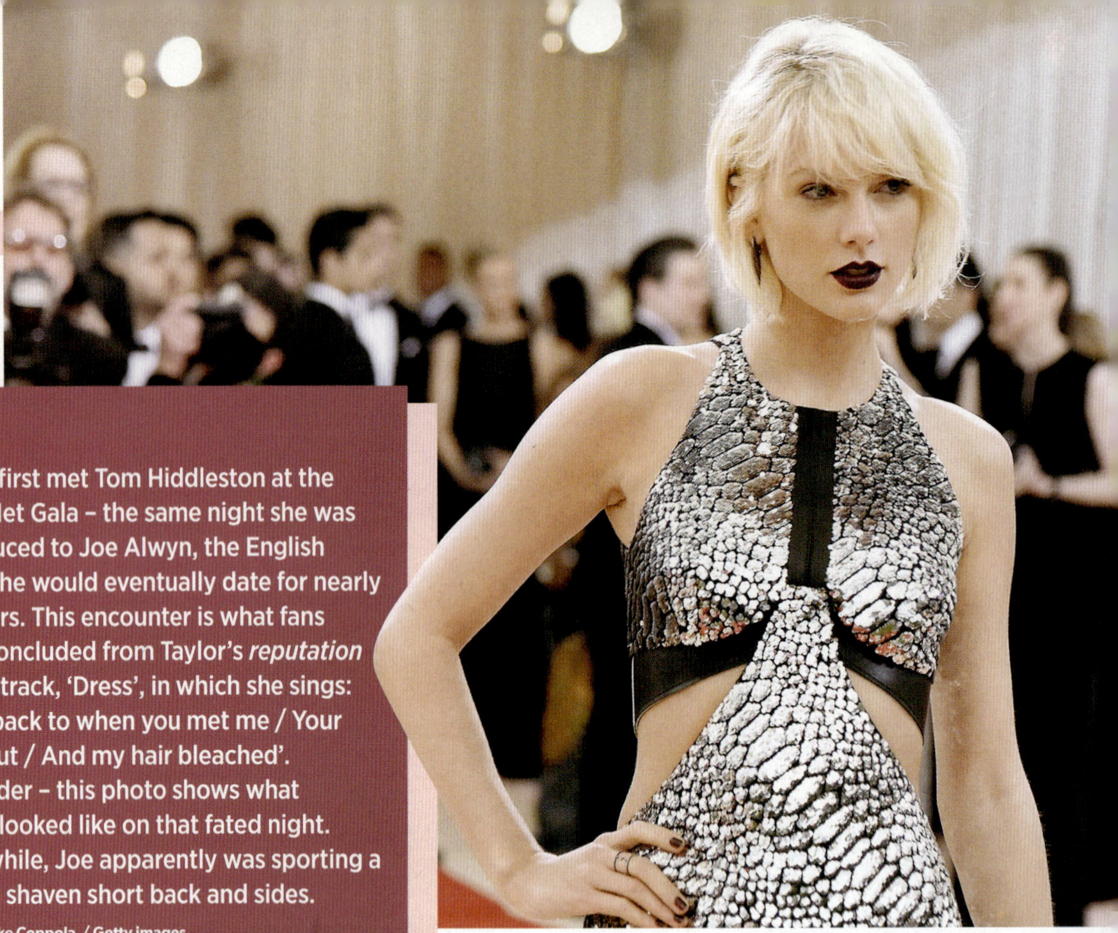

LOVER

▶ Taylor first met Tom Hiddleston at the 2016 Met Gala – the same night she was introduced to Joe Alwyn, the English actor she would eventually date for nearly six years. This encounter is what fans have concluded from Taylor's *reputation* album track, 'Dress', in which she sings: 'Flashback to when you met me / Your buzz cut / And my hair bleached'. Reminder – this photo shows what Taylor looked like on that fated night. Meanwhile, Joe apparently was sporting a freshly shaven short back and sides.

Image: Mike Coppola / Getty images

▼ News broke in May 2017 – a whole year after the Met Gala – that Taylor was dating Joe. Two years after this, engagement rumours were sparked when Taylor's album, *Lover*, alluded to marriage, but neither party confirmed nor denied the rumours. In fact, compared to previous relationships, Taylor's romance with Joe was kept well out of the public eye.

Image: Christopher Polk / Getty images

▲ Despite keeping her relationship with Joe away from the prying eyes of the press, Taylor still included a variety of subtle and not-so subtle references to the *Conversations with Friends* actor in her music. The track 'London Boy' from *Lover* clearly relates to the actor, as she namechecks city haunts where they've hung out. Joe even collaborated with Taylor on some tracks for her lockdown albums, *folklore* and *evermore* – he's just credited under the pseudonym William Bowery.

Image: Ricky Vigil M / Getty images

One thing that has been a constant in Taylor's life is her friendship with Abigail Anderson. The BFFs hit it off when they were just 15 years old during their freshman year at Henderson High School in Tennessee. Not only did Abigail inspire the lyrics of Taylor's hit 'Fifteen', but she also appeared in the song's music video. Taylor has even been her best pal's bridesmaid.

Image: Lester Cohen / WireImage / Getty images

Sadly, Taylor's six-year romance with Joe was not meant to be. Reports surfaced in April 2023 that the couple had amicably called it quits. A source told *Entertainment Today* that "the relationship had just run its course". At the time of going to print, Taylor was reportedly dating Matt Healy, the lead vocalist of band the 1975, pictured left.

Image: Emma McIntyre / WireImage / Getty images

ONE CONSTANT IN TAYLOR'S LIFE IS HER FRIENDSHIP WITH ABIGAIL ANDERSON

LOVER

SELENA GOMEZ AND TAYLOR NOW HAVE ONE OF THE STRONGEST FRIENDSHIPS IN THE MUSIC INDUSTRY

Selena Gomez and Taylor met when they were both dating Jonas brothers in 2008, and now have one of the strongest friendships in the music industry. From hyping each other's music to performing on stage together, they have never stopped publicly supporting one another. Speaking about Taylor in March 2023, Selena said: "She's a role model. I don't think that's something you sign up for; I just think it's something you inherently have inside of you, and I think that's Taylor."

Image: Keven Mazur / Getty images

Did you know?

THE FRIENDSHIP BETWEEN BLAKE LIVELY AND TAYLOR JUST KEEPS GETTING SWEETER. THE BESTIES FIRST MET IN 2014 AND HAVE BEEN HANGING OUT AT PARTIES AND POSTING PICS TOGETHER ON SOCIAL MEDIA EVER SINCE. TAYLOR EVEN SAMPLED BLAKE'S ELDEST DAUGHTER, JAMES, ON HER 2017 SONG 'GORGEOUS'. THEN IN 2020, TAYLOR NAMECHECKED JAMES AND HER TWO YOUNGER SISTERS, INEZ AND BETTY, IN HER SONG 'BETTY' ON HER *FOLKLORE* ALBUM. RECENTLY, BLAKE AND HER HUSBAND RYAN REYNOLDS GAVE UP THEIR LAKESIDE HOME FOR TAYLOR TO USE AS THE SET FOR HER *ALL TOO WELL* SHORT FILM, WHILE THE *GOSSIP GIRL* ACTOR DIRECTED THE MUSIC VIDEO FOR 'I BET YOU THINK ABOUT ME (TAYLOR'S VERSION)' IN 2021.

Image: Theo Wargo / WireImage / Getty Images

- The Swift Squad slowly vanished from the public consciousness. An explanation for its disappearance came in 2019, when Taylor wrote an essay for *Elle* magazine in which she mused about outgrowing the friendships she had in her twenties. She also apologised for being so in-your-face-about the girl gang. No names were dropped, but she said how surrounding herself with a clique of friends had come from insecurities she had as a kid about not having any friends. The squad had drawn criticism for being made up of impossibly skinny, mainly white women and for the elitism this entailed.

Image: Kevin Mazur / LP5 / WireImage / Getty images

LOVER

As Taylor's success skyrocketed, she began to amass more and more celebrity pals. The large yet close-knit circle of friends was dubbed the 'Swift Squad' by the media and included a roll call of in-demand models and actor, including Gigi Hadid, Kendall Jenner, Cara Delevingne, Lily Aldridge, Martha Hunt and Karlie Kloss. During her 1989 Tour, squad members would make surprise appearances on stage and even featured as an ensemble cast in her 2014 single, 'Bad Blood'.

Image: Steve Granitz / WireImage / Getty images

LOVER

TAYLOR SENT THEM A SATIN PINK BLANKET SHE MADE HERSELF

There was a time when Karlie Kloss and Taylor appeared inseparable. Soon after appearing together at the 2014 Victoria's Secret Fashion Show, the pals solidified their friendship with a well-documented road trip to the Big Sur. Over the years, it appears the pair have drifted apart. While the model asserts they remain good friends, Taylor has stayed silent on the matter. Karlie has been hanging out with Scooter Braun, after all.

Image: Tim P. Whitby / Getty images

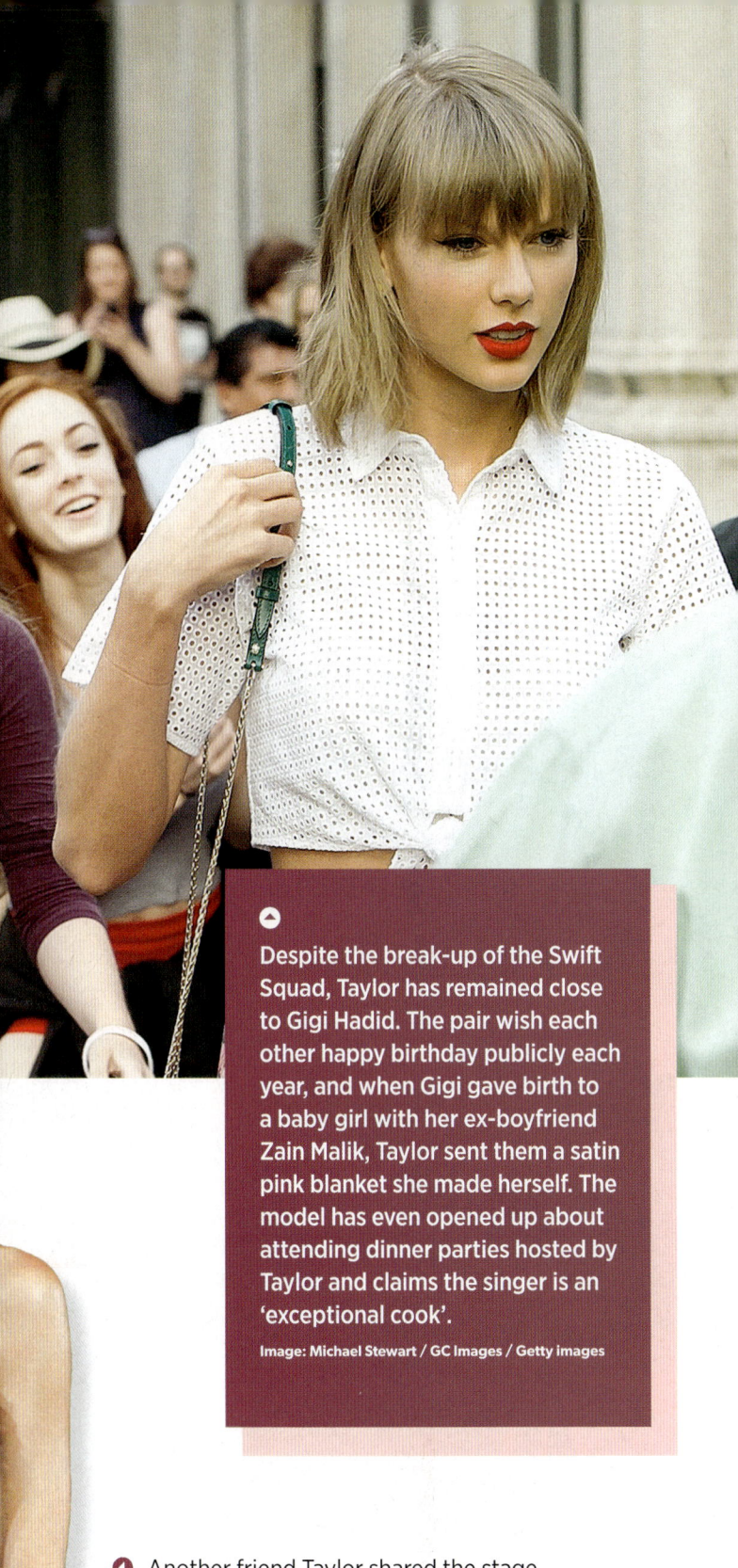

Despite the break-up of the Swift Squad, Taylor has remained close to Gigi Hadid. The pair wish each other happy birthday publicly each year, and when Gigi gave birth to a baby girl with her ex-boyfriend Zain Malik, Taylor sent them a satin pink blanket she made herself. The model has even opened up about attending dinner parties hosted by Taylor and claims the singer is an 'exceptional cook'.

Image: Michael Stewart / GC Images / Getty images

Another friend Taylor shared the stage with during her 1989 World Tour was New Zealand artist Lorde. The 'Royales' singer was taken under Taylor's wing and even appeared in her 'Bad Blood' video. Yet Lorde's close relationship to producer Jack Antonoff allegedly caused a rift between the two friends, especially as Taylor is great pals with Lena Dunham, who was Jack's long-term girlfriend at the time.

Image: Kris Connor / LP5 / Getty images

Fun Fact

TAYLOR JOKED SHE WAS OFFICIALLY THE 'FOURTH HAIM SISTER' AFTER COLLABORATING WITH THE BAND ON A REMIX OF THEIR TRACK 'GASOLINE' IN 2021. BUT THE SINGER'S FRIENDSHIP WITH ALANA, DANIELLE AND ESTE HAIM GOES WAY BACK TO 2014, WITH REPORTS OF SEVEN-HOUR-LONG DINNERS, FOURTH OF JULY PARTIES AND PIZZA-FUELLED SLEEPOVERS TOGETHER. THE BAND EVEN OPENED FOR TAYLOR ON HER 1989 WORLD TOUR AND EIGHT YEARS LATER ON THE ERAS TOUR. IN THE INTERIM, TAYLOR JOINED HAIM ON STAGE AT THE O2 IN LONDON TO PERFORM A MASH UP OF 'LOVE STORY' AND 'GASOLINE', WHERE ALL FOUR MUSICIANS WORE THE SAME BLACK LEATHER TROUSERS (PICTURED HERE). PLUS, 'NO BODY, NO CRIME' ON *EVERMORE* FEATURES GUEST VOCALS FROM HAIM, WITH THE CENTRAL CHARACTER NAMED AFTER ESTE HAIM, AS SHE IS A TRUE CRIME OBSESSIVE.

Image: Nicky J Sims / Getty Images

LOVER

▸ After meeting at a Golden Globes party in 2014, Taylor and actor, Jaime King, have forged a friendship for life. Taylor was even made a godmother to Jaime's son Leo. Explaining why she picked the singer for the role, the *Hart of Dixie* actor said: "I see what she gives out there to her fans and to her family and that's the kind of person I want to be the guide and the spiritual protector of my child."

Image: Michael Kovac / Getty images

Fun Fact

Around 12 months after breaking up with Calvin Harris, Taylor was uncovered as co-writer of his smash hit with Rhianna, 'This Is What You Came For'. An unnamed source claims Taylor wrote the song at her piano before sending an iPhone recording to Calvin. The then-couple then did a full demo in the studio with Taylor on vocals and Calvin creating the beats – the same demo leaked by a supposed hacker in March 2023. On the final version, Taylor's backing vocals are uncredited, but she is credited as a writer, just under the pseudonym of 'Nils Sjöberg'.

Image: Kevin Mazur / Getty Images

LOVER

After breaking up with Calvin Harris, Taylor was uncovered as co-writer of his smash hit

A friend who goes even further back is actor Emma Stone. She's been tight with Taylor ever since the pair started exchanging emails (yes, it was that long ago!) back in 2009. At one of the pop star's recent Eras Tour concerts, the *Cruella* and *La La Land* actor was spotted in full-on Swiftie mode jamming to 'You Belong to Me' in the VIP section of the arena.

Image: John Shearer / WireImage / Getty images

Despite much internet speculation, Ed Sheeran and Taylor have never dated – they've just been giving us friendship goals since penning the song 'Everything Has Changed' together for Taylor's 2012 album, *RED*. 'The Lego House' singer then opened for Taylor on some RED tour dates, and after gifting each other jam and drinking out of personalised mugs together, the pair duetted again on 'End Game' in 2017 and, most recently, for the remix of Ed's 'The Joker And The Queen'.

Image: Kevin Mazur / WireImage / Getty images

Ever since the release of her debut album, Taylor has shown her fans a lot of love. From leaving secret messages in album covers to hosting post-show hangouts and marathon meet-and-greets, she has amassed a loyal army of Swifties, whose support only continues to grow.

Image: Dave Hogan / TAS / Getty images

THE BOND TAYLOR SHARES WITH HER FANS HAS EVOLVED INTO SOMETHING MORE LIKE FRIENDSHIP

LOVER

Taylor's generosity knows no bounds when it comes to her fans. She's been reported to surprise Swifties in their own homes, gift huge packages complete with personalised notes, help pay off student loans and deliver Christmas care packages – remember #Swiftmas anyone? Other acts of kindness include regular visits to sick fans in hospital, donating $10,000 for a service dog for a boy with autism and buying a house for a pregnant fan in financial need.

Image: Kevin Mazur / WireImage / Getty images

The bond Taylor shares with her fans has evolved into something more like friendship. This is partly down to the personal and intimate ways she communicates with them, whether it's posting a video on TikTok or broadcasting via Instagram Live. She also comes up with endlessly fascinating ways to keep her fans invested, from hiding Easter eggs in her social media to recruiting Swifties to dance alongside her in the music video for 'Shake It Off'.

Image: Gareth Cattermole / TAS18 / Getty images

LOVER

▶ Seen here with young ambassadors from Save the Children at Westfield Shopping Centre in London, where she performed a mini-concert, Taylor donates time and funds to charities. She regularly volunteers with the Make-A-Wish Foundation too, while she was moved to write the song 'Ronan' for Maya Thompson, a fan who lost her four-year-old boy Ronan to cancer in 2011.
Image: David M. Benett / Getty images

SHE IS ALWAYS CHAMPIONING LOCAL CAUSES

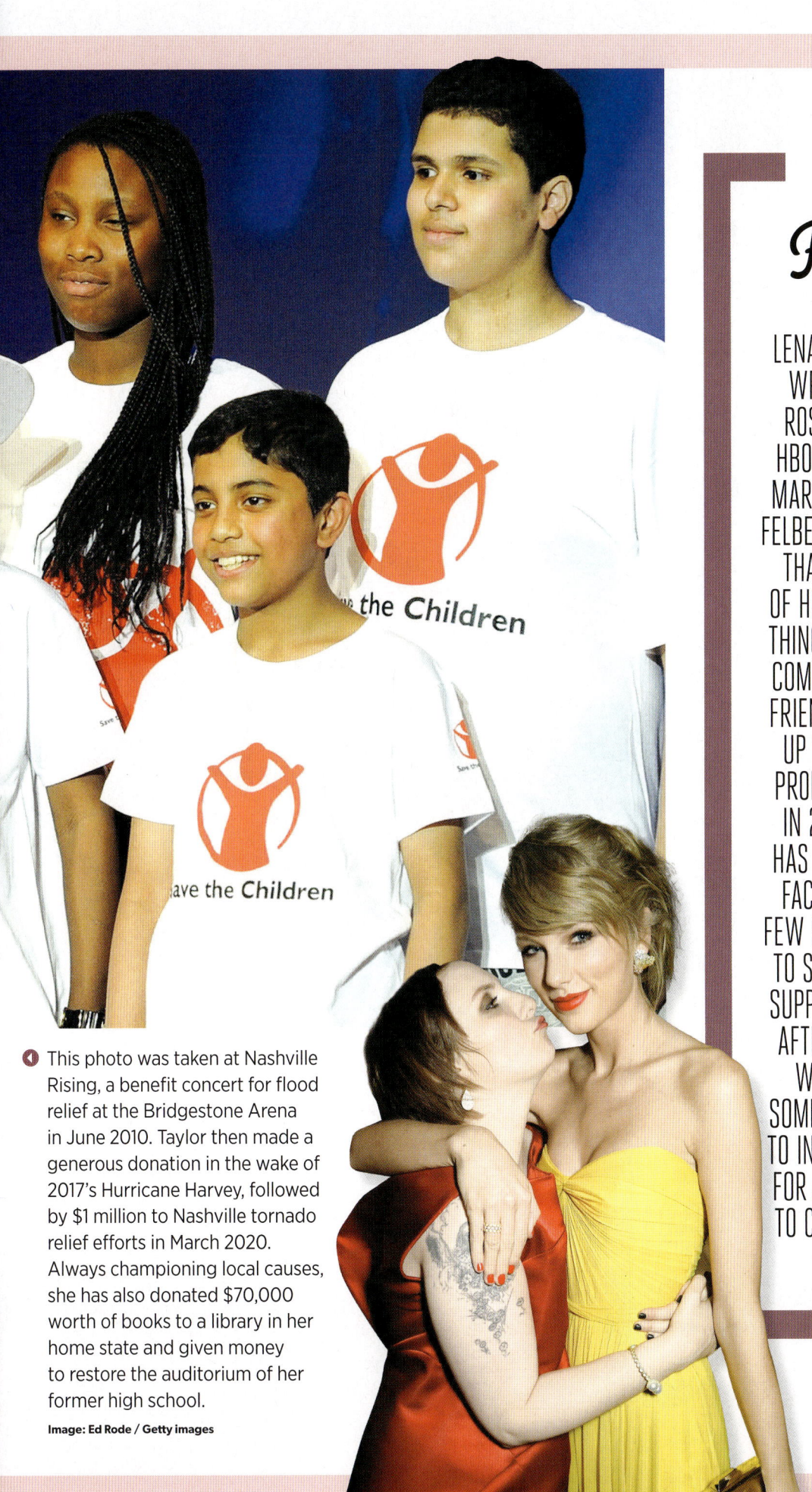

○ This photo was taken at Nashville Rising, a benefit concert for flood relief at the Bridgestone Arena in June 2010. Taylor then made a generous donation in the wake of 2017's Hurricane Harvey, followed by $1 million to Nashville tornado relief efforts in March 2020. Always championing local causes, she has also donated $70,000 worth of books to a library in her home state and given money to restore the auditorium of her former high school.

Image: Ed Rode / Getty images

Fun Fact

LENA DUNHAM, THE ACTOR-WRITER-DIRECTOR WHO ROSE TO FAME WITH HER HBO DRAMA *GIRLS*, IS NOW MARRIED TO MUSICIAN LUIS FELBER AND HAD NONE OTHER THAN PAL TAYLOR AS ONE OF HER EIGHT BRIDESMAIDS. THINGS COULD HAVE GOTTEN COMPLICATED FOR THE TWO FRIENDS WHEN LENA BROKE UP WITH TAYLOR'S MUSIC PRODUCER JACK ANTONOFF IN 2018, BUT THEIR BOND HAS PROVED INVINCIBLE. IN FACT, LENA IS ONE OF THE FEW SWIFT SQUAD MEMBERS TO STAND BY AND PUBLICLY SUPPORT THE SINGER IN THE AFTERMATH OF THE KANYE WEST CONTROVERSY – SOMETHING TAYLOR ALLUDED TO IN THE ESSAY SHE WROTE FOR *ELLE* MAGAZINE IN 2019 TO CELEBRATE TURNING 30.

Image: Jeff Kravitz / Getty Images

Did you know?

INTEREST INTO WHAT ACTUALLY WENT ON BETWEEN TAYLOR AND JAKE GYLLENHAAL WAS RECENTLY REIGNITED. IT WAS ALL DOWN TO THE RE-RELEASE OF *RED*, THE ALBUM TAYLOR HAS SINCE CLAIMED IS 'ABOUT A PURE, ABSOLUTE, TO THE CORE HEARTBREAK' WITH THE MARVEL ACTOR BELIEVED TO BE THE SOURCE OF SUCH DISCONTENT. HERE TAYLOR PERFORMS HER NEW VERSION OF 'ALL TOO WELL' ON *SATURDAY NIGHT LIVE* IN NOVEMBER 2021. WHEN ASKED ABOUT HIS THOUGHTS ON THE ALBUM, JAKE GRACIOUSLY REPLIED: "IT HAS NOTHING TO DO WITH ME. IT'S ABOUT HER RELATIONSHIP WITH HER FANS. IT IS HER EXPRESSION. ARTISTS TAP INTO PERSONAL EXPERIENCES FOR INSPIRATION, AND I DON'T BEGRUDGE ANYONE THAT."

Image: Will Heath / NBC / NBCU / Getty Images

▶ While undertaking The Eras Tour in 2023, Taylor made quiet donations to food banks along the way. This generosity was not publicised by the singer, but by the food banks in Arizona and Nevada, which shared the story with local news outlets. Taylor then revealed how she wanted to make a positive impact in the communities where she was touring.

Image: John Shearer / Getty images

LOVER

TAYLOR REVEALED HOW SHE WANTED TO MAKE A POSITIVE IMPACT IN THE COMMUNITIES WHERE SHE WAS TOURING

Taylor also uses her platform to increase awareness of causes she cares about. Here she performs at Children in Need, helping raise money for disadvantaged kids. Then during the pandemic, she sang at the 'One World: Together at Home' benefit in 2020, as well as making donations to fans who tweeted about the financial struggles they were experiencing due to Covid 19.

Image: PA Images / Getty images

REPUTATION

HOW TAYLOR SWIFT WENT FROM COUNTRY STARLET TO GLOBAL SUPERSTAR

REPUTAT

REPUTATION

ION

REPUTATION

Taylor was just a fresh-faced 16-year-old when she released her self-titled, debut album. Written by the starlet while she was still in high school, the tracks tell the story of a small-town American teenager. But the girl-next-door package proved insanely popular, as Taylor's fresh country sound and autobiographical narratives on romance, friendship and insecurities resonated with audiences across the US and beyond.

Image: Ethan Miller / Getty images

Embarking on a six-month radio tour, Taylor worked tirelessly to promote her first album after it was released in 2006. As her reputation grew, she even got to open for some big country names she admired, including Brad Paisley, Kenny Chesney, and Tim McGraw and Faith Hill. The young singer would then go on to perform alongside her idols later in her career. She's pictured on stage here with Faith Hill in 2010.

Image: Frederick Breedon / WireImage / Getty images

Fun Fact

SWIFTIES SINCE THE BEGINNING WILL KNOW TAYLOR INCLUDED HIDDEN MESSAGES IN THE CD LINERS OF HER FIRST FIVE ALBUMS. SEEMINGLY RANDOM CAPITAL LETTERS IN THE LYRIC BOOKLETS WHEN PUT TOGETHER SPELL OUT PHRASES THAT PROVIDE CLUES FOR THE SUBJECT OF EVERY SONG. FOR EXAMPLE, IN THE LYRIC SHEET FOR *FEARLESS*, TAYLOR CAPITALISED LETTERS THAT SPELT OUT 'I CRIED WHILE RECORDING THIS' FOR THE SONG 'FIFTEEN'. FOR THE HIT SONG '22' ON HER ALBUM *RED*, THE CAPITAL LETTERS SPELL OUT 'ASHLEY DIANNA CLAIRE SELENA', A REFERENCE TO HER BFFS AT THE TIME. MESSAGES ON *1989* INCLUDE 'SHE DANCED TO FORGET HIM' FOR 'SHAKE IT OFF' AND 'SHE MADE FRIENDS AND ENEMIES' FOR 'BAD BLOOD'.

Image: Kevin Mazur / TCA / Getty Images

REPUTATION

FEARLESS HAD MAJOR CROSSOVER APPEAL, CATAPULTING TAYLOR INTO THE MAINSTREAM

▸ When Taylor's second album, *Fearless*, arrived in November 2008, she had already reached headliner status. Starting her first ever concert tour in Indiana in April 2009, she performed across North America, Europe, Australia and Asia. Following on from its predecessor, *Fearless* had major crossover appeal, catapulting Taylor out of the country charts and into the mainstream.

Image: Jason Kempin / Getty images

REPUTATION

▶ Having written or co-written all the album tracks on *Fearless*, Taylor brought in fairy-tale imagery, such as princesses, princes and white horses, to explore falling in love and starry-eyed romances. The lead single, 'Love Story', is about a troubled romance ending in a marriage proposal with references to Shakespeare's *Romeo and Juliet*, hence the red, Elizabethan-style dress she wore while performing the track on tour.

Image: Jason Kempin / Getty images

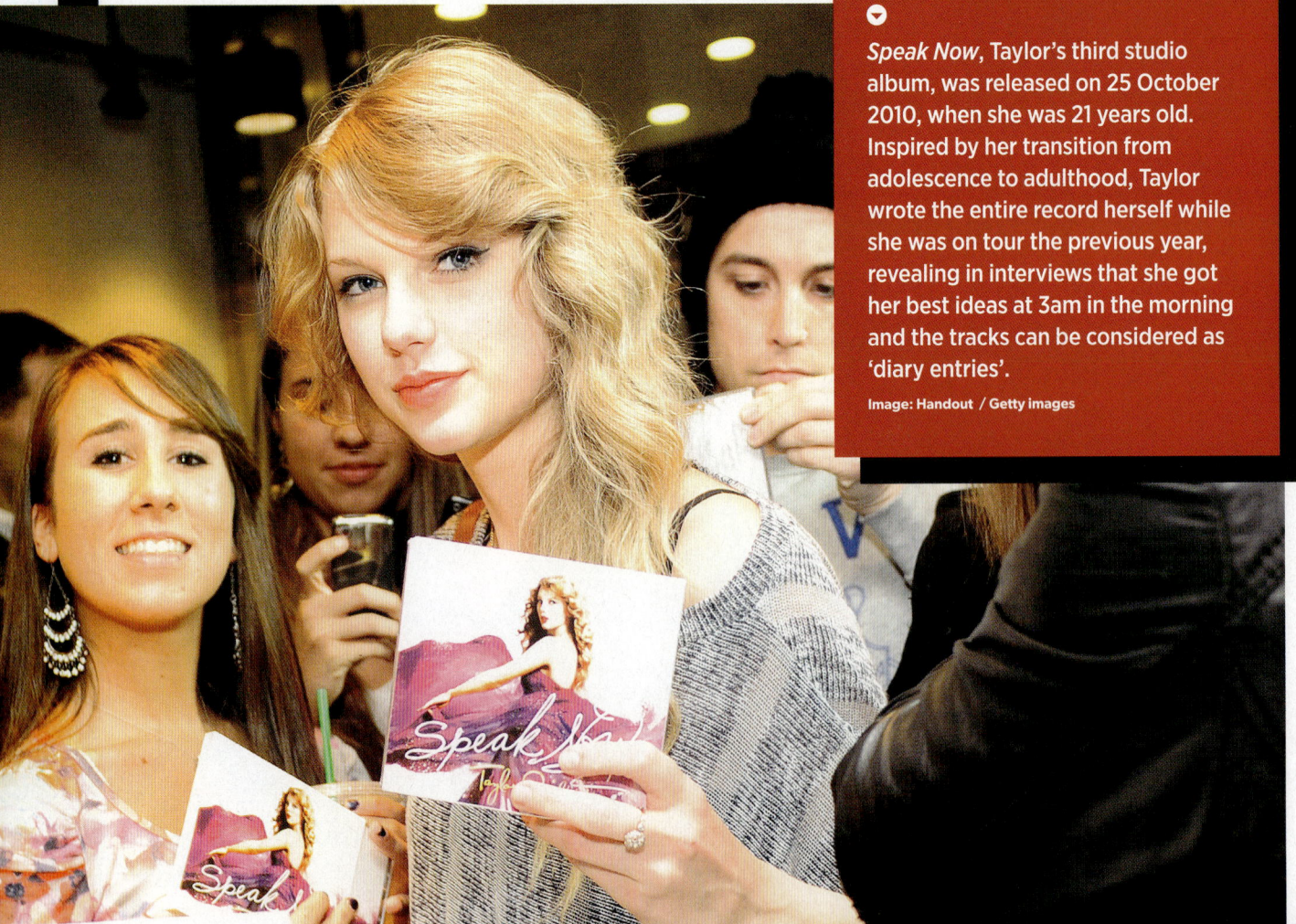

▶ *Speak Now*, Taylor's third studio album, was released on 25 October 2010, when she was 21 years old. Inspired by her transition from adolescence to adulthood, Taylor wrote the entire record herself while she was on tour the previous year, revealing in interviews that she got her best ideas at 3am in the morning and the tracks can be considered as 'diary entries'.

Image: Handout / Getty images

REPUTATION

● Love and heartache are still very much central themes in Taylor's third album, but a few songs explore her new experiences of being in the public eye. Now known for her trademark blend of country and pop, she began the Speak Now World Tour in early 2011, performing in stadiums for the very first time. Here she's seen performing at the LG Arena in Birmingham, England.

Image: Dave Hogan / Getty images

LOVE AND HEARTACHE ARE STILL VERY MUCH CENTRAL THEMES TO TAYLOR'S THIRD ALBUM

● Not only did *Fearless* bring Taylor legions of new fans and commercial success, it also wowed music industry insiders. Selling 3.217 million copies in the US alone in 2009, the album won Grammys for the Best Country Album and Album of the Year, making Taylor, who was 20 at the time, the youngest artist to ever win the award.

Image: Kevin Winter / Getty images

65

Iconic imagery from the RED Tour will forever be associated with her hits from the album, 'We Are Never Ever Getting Back Together' and 'I Knew You Were Trouble'. Laying bare her emotional life, she was beginning to outgrow her public image of an innocent sweetheart, as well as contemplate themes such as one's perceived image and the pressures of fame.

Image: Nicky Loh / Getty images

Taylor's fourth album, RED, moves away from the fantasy-driven narratives and happy endings of her previous work. Released in autumn 2012, the record faces up to the stark reality that love can sometimes come to a messy, painful end, with the title referring to the tumultuous 'red' emotions she felt during the album's conception, evoked by unhealthy romantic relationships.

Image: Larry Bussaca / Getty images

Did you know?

BEFORE EVERY SHOW ON THE AMERICAN AND AUSTRALIAN LEGS OF HER SPEAK NOW WORLD TOUR, TAYLOR WOULD WRITE SONG LYRICS ON HER LEFT ARM WITH A BLACK SHARPIE. BUT THEY WEREN'T LYRICS OF HER OWN CREATION. INSTEAD, THE INSPIRING LINES WERE TAKEN FROM SONGS THAT SPOKE TO HER FROM DIFFERENT ARTISTS, RANGING FROM FELLOW COUNTRY STARS FAITH HILL AND THE DIXIE CHICKS TO ROCKERS U2 AND TOM PETTY. SHE EVEN PENNED LINES FROM BEST FRIEND SELENA GOMEZ'S HITS 'WHO SAYS' AND 'GHOST OF YOU'. TAYLOR TOLD FANS THE WORDS SHOULD BE VIEWED AS A NIGHTLY 'MOOD RING' AS SHE PICKED THE SONG DEPENDING ON HOW SHE FELT THAT DAY.

Image: Larry Busacca / Getty Images

REPUTATION

The RED Tour made history when it grossed $150 million – the highest amount ever for a county artist. But Taylor was making a gradual transition to pop, with *RED* showcasing a range of musical styles Taylor called a 'metaphor for how messy a real break up is'. It required the star to venture outside of her comfort zone by collaborating with new producers and other musicians – such as Ed Sheeran who provided guest vocals on the track 'Everything Has Changed'.

Image: Gareth Cattermole / TAS / Getty images

REPUTATION

Following the pop- and electronic-influenced *RED*, Taylor's status as a country musician was already being questioned. But the release of the singer's *1989* album in October 2014 well and truly cemented her status as a pop star. The name of this fifth album, which is Taylor's year of birth, signifies her symbolic re-birth as she worked with renowned pop producers Max Martin and Shellback, and brought a fiercer look to her stage shows.

Image: Christopher Polk / Getty images

REPUTATION

THE RELEASE OF THE SINGER'S 1989 ALBUM IN OCTOBER 2014 WELL AND TRULY CEMENTED HER STATUS AS A POP STAR

● Expanding on her song-writing skills, Taylor took inspiration from her personal life for the tracks on *RED*. Unlike previous albums, she did not villainise past lovers but wrote from a perspective. Coming under scrutiny from the tabloids, she also used the album as an opportunity to satirise the media's perception of her as a serial dater in songs such as 'Blank Space' and 'Shake It Off' – which won Song of the Year at the iHeartRadio Music Awards in 2015.

Image: Kevin Mazur / Getty images

REPUTATION

▶ The 1989 World Tour became the highest grossing tour in 2015, with critics praising the production and Taylor's mesmerising stage presence. Her performances will also be remembered for the appearances of unannounced special guests, which included a roll call of her celeb friends including the likes of Cara Delevingne, Kendall Jenner, Karlie Kloss, Martha Hunt and Gigi Hadid.

Image: Brian Rasic / LP5 / Getty images

▼ After her 1989 World Tour, Taylor disappeared from the public eye to avoid the media's increasing scrutiny and frenzy about her private life and the infamous fall out between the singer and Kanye West. Taking a bigger break than normal between records, she was back in the autumn of 2017 with her sixth studio album, *reputation*. The star refused to speak to the press, but drag racer Courtney Force competed on track with the album imagery plastered on her Chevrolet Camaro.

Image: David Becker / Getty images

Fun Fact

Leaving secret messages in the CD liners of her albums was just the beginning for Taylor. For over a decade now, she's become a master at dropping cryptic clues and hidden messages for her fans to decipher and admits she "loves to communicate through Easter eggs". During her *Reputation* era, this involved planting 'thousands' of visual Easter eggs into the video for 'Look What You Made Me Do', nodding to her rivals and past scandals. While the music video for 2019 single 'ME!' featuring Brendon Urie of Panic! At The Disco (seen performing together here) hinted at her next album's title – you can see the words 'Lover' appear at the 1.56 timestamp in the video.

Image: Kevin Winter / Getty Images

REPUTATION

Just before *reputation's* launch, Taylor generated a huge amount of speculation by clearing her website and social media accounts of content. The hype paid off as fans were introduced to a darker side of the singer. Not only is the electropop sound of the album far heavier than her previously bright and breezy tracks, but the lyrics also deal with grittier topics such as vengeance, the downside of fame and the resultant anger.

Image: Alexander Tamargo / Getty images

FOR OVER A DECADE NOW, SHE'S BECOME A MASTER AT DROPPING CRYPTIC CLUES AND HIDDEN MESSAGES

REPUTATION

Taylor would reinvent herself again with the release of her seventh studio album, *Lover*. Pictured here introducing the record in Brooklyn, New York, Taylor unleashed a newfound creativity to write the tracks after recalibrating her personal life and freeing herself from her public image. As a result, the record features bright, light-hearted vibes with confessional and playful songs about love and emotional intimacy.

Image: Gotham / Getty images

Taylor told *Rolling Stone* in 2019 that she conceptualised *Lover* as "just a barn wood floor and some ripped curtains flowing in the breeze, and fields of flowers". Unfortunately Covid-19 scuppered her touring plans, so fans didn't see how her seventh album would be brought to life. But tracks from the album featured in the set list of her 2023 Eras Tour, pictured here.

Image: Omar Vega / TAS23 / Getty images

REPUTATION

Taylor told *Rolling Stone* that she conceptualised *reputation* as a "night-time cityscape" with "old warehouse buildings that had been deserted". This, together with the themes of the album, were in the stage production for the reputation Stadium Tour, pictured here. Incorporating goth subculture, snake motifs and Broadway theatricality, it became the highest ever grossing tour in North America by a female artist.

Image: Don Arnold / Getty images

TAYLOR UNLEASHED A NEWFOUND CREATIVITY TO WRITE THE TRACKS

Lover won the Favourite Album award at the 2019 American Music Awards and became the best selling global album of the year by a solo artist. Most of the tracks were recorded in New York with Taylor's long-term collaborator Jack Antonoff, whose production is characterised by 1980s drums, atmospheric synthesisers, and reverbed beats. The vocals were recorded as if Taylor was performing live, with the majority of the tracks said to be full takes.

Image: JC Olivera / Getty images

Swifties were ecstatic when Taylor released a surprise album in July 2020 called *folklore*, which went on to win a Grammy for Album of the Year. On stage with Taylor are producers Jack Antonoff and Aaron Dessner, who she worked with virtually – due to the Covid-19 quarantine measures – to record the album. In Taylor's own words, *folklore* is "a collection of songs and stories that flowed like a stream of consciousness".

Image: Kevin Winter / Getty images

REPUTATION

▲ Taylor treated audiences at the 2021 Grammy Awards to an acoustic performance of three tracks from folklore. Departing from the upbeat pop of Taylor's previous albums, folklore features mellow ballads, taking inspiration from indie folk, alternative rock and electroacoustic styles. Exploring escapism, empathy and nostalgia, the record also diverts from the singer's back catalogue by swapping autobiographical details for a new rota of characters and story arcs.

Image: TAS Rights Management 2021 / Getty images

THE RECORD SWAPS AUTOBIOGRAPHICAL DETAILS FOR NEW CHARACTERS AND STORY ARCS

Did you know?

TAYLOR WENT IN HEAVY WITH THE SNAKE IMAGERY DURING HER REPUTATION TOUR. FROM A MECHANISED COBRA TO SNAKE MERCHANDISE, SNAKE-EMBROIDERED CLOTHING AND A SNAKE MICROPHONE, THE REPTILIAN CREATURE WAS EVERYWHERE. IT WAS PART OF TAYLOR'S PLOY TO RECLAIM THE MOTIF AFTER BEING CALLED A SNAKE BY KIM KARDASHIAN, FOLLOWING A FEUD WITH THE REALITY TV STAR AND HER THEN HUSBAND, KANYE WEST. AFTER BEING HOUNDED BY SOCIAL MEDIA USERS WITH THE SNAKE EMOJI, THE REPUTATION TOUR WAS TAYLOR'S STAND AGAINST THE ONLINE BULLIES. OF THE SITUATION, SHE SAID: "I LEARNED A REALLY IMPORTANT LESSON THAT I'VE BEEN TELLING YOU FROM THE STAGE FOR ABOUT TEN YEARS, BUT I NEVER HAD TO LEARN IT SO HARSHLY MYSELF – AND THAT LESSON HAS TO DO WITH HOW MUCH YOU VALUE YOUR REPUTATION."

Image: Don Arnold / TAS18 / Getty Images

REPUTATION

Another surprise album, *evermore*, arrived in December 2020 five months after *folklore*. Both lockdown albums are said to be sister projects, but Taylor explained in an Apple Music interview that while *folklore* deals with "conflict resolution", *evermore* explores "endings of all sorts, sizes and shapes" and the pain and phases of such closures. Combining indie folk with chamber pop styles, Taylor again wowed fans worldwide.

Image: Mark Metcalfe / Getty images

In *Midnights*, Taylor returns to her first-person storytelling. Calling it a story of "13 sleepless nights scattered throughout my life", the album abounds with confessional yet cryptic lyrics, exploring themes such as self-hatred, revenge fantasies, wondering what might have been, falling in love and falling apart. Expanding on the synth-pop of her previous albums, the songs experiment with subtle grooves, vintage synthesisers and chill-out music.

Image: Mike Kemp / Getty images

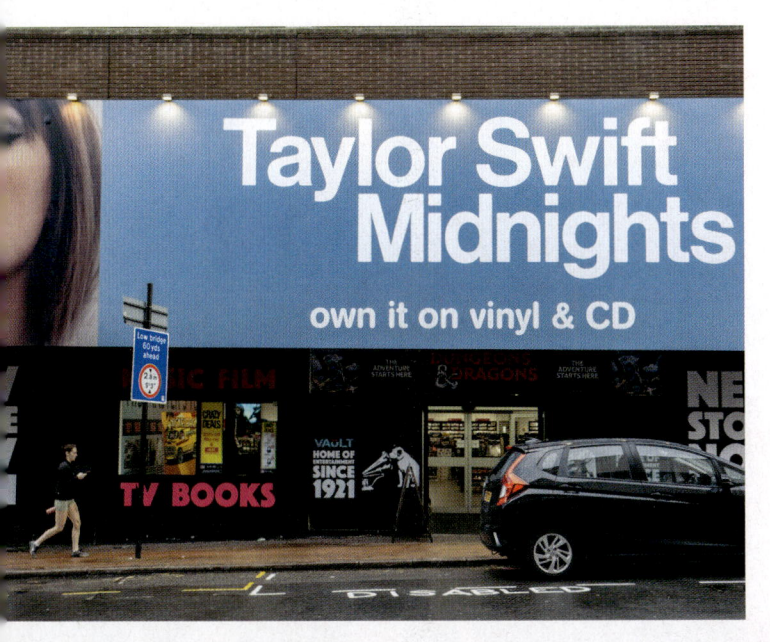

Taylor announced the release of her tenth studio album, *Midnights* – at midnight. It followed the 2022 MTV VMA, where she wore a navy blue Moschino dress embroidered with silver stars to an after party, subtly hinting at the name of her fifth album in three years. It went on to become the singer's most commercially successful album.

Image: Gotham / Getty images

REPUTATION

> In April 2022, Taylor released a re-recording of her second studio album, with the title *Fearless (Taylor's version)*. Although the album was praised by critics and fans alike, it was not created under the best of circumstances, as it followed a dispute over the ownership of the masters to Taylor's first six studio albums. The promotional campaign included a prime billboard spot in New York's Times Square.

Image: Noam Galai / Getty images

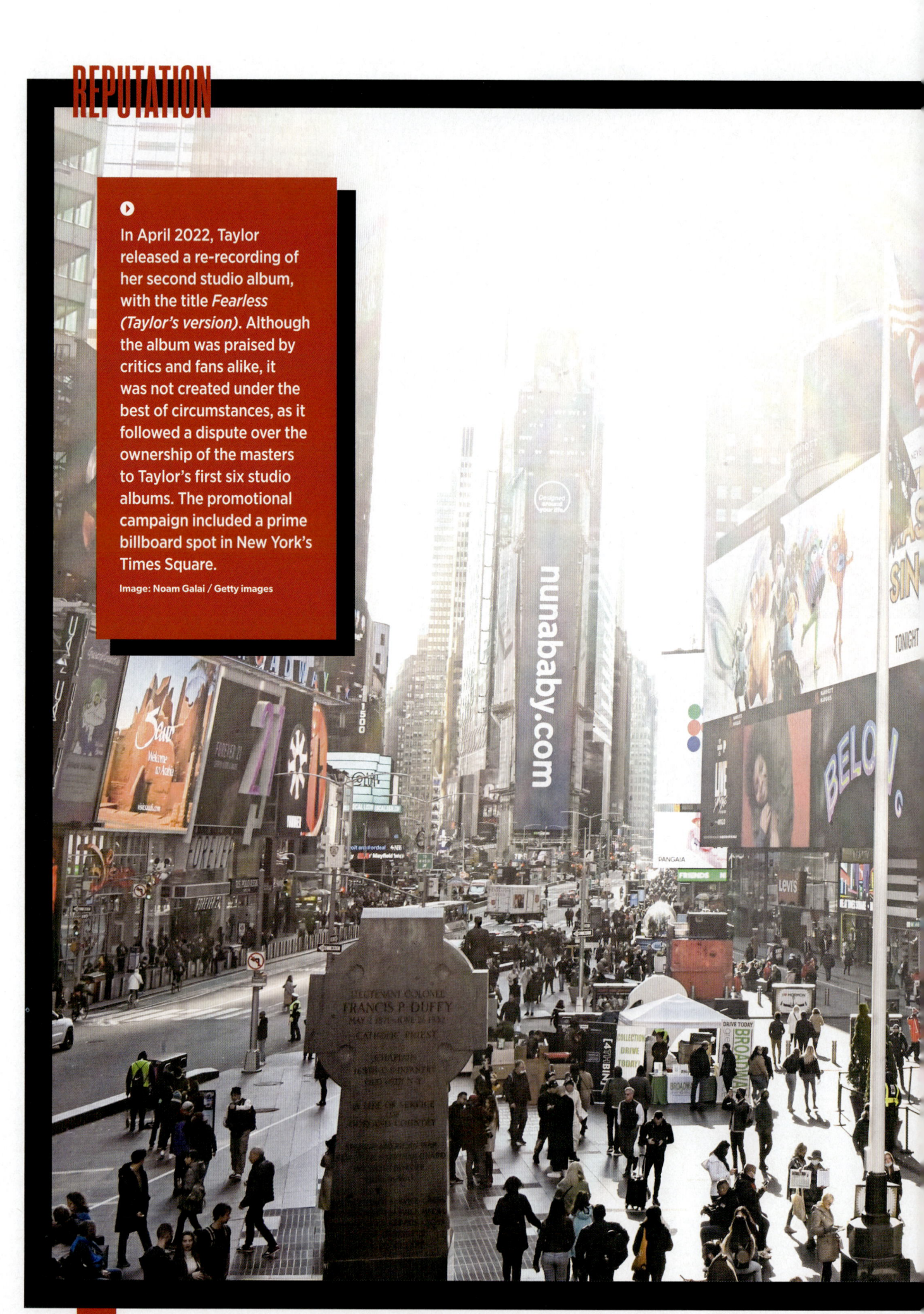

REPUTATION

REPUTATION

- Seven months later, Taylor released the second of her re-recorded albums, *RED (Taylor's Version)*, as part of her countermeasure against the purchase of her back catalogue. The album's 30 tracks are made up of 20 from the deluxe edition of RED, as well as previously unreleased 'from-the-vault' offerings. Ed Sheeran and Gary Lightbody even returned to provide guest vocals, and it racked up even more awards and accolades, such as Favourite Pop Album at the 2022 American Music Awards.

Image: Matt Winkelmeyer / Getty images

- After the Covid-19 pandemic put a halt to Taylor's Lover Tour, she decided to change the focus of her stadium visits in 2023. Called the Eras Tour, the 44-song set list took concert-goers on a journey through Taylor's musical eras, serving as a reminder of how Taylor began as a Nashville country starlet and rose to become a musical superstar, overcoming intense media scrutiny about her personal life, public fallouts and feuds, and music ownership controversy along the way.

Image: Ethan Miller /TAS23 / Getty images

Fun Fact

Although unlucky for some, the number 13 is Taylor's favourite – she even went through a phrase of drawing it onto her hand (sometimes in eyeliner) before her big stage performances. When interviewed about the significance of the number, the connections turned out to be uncanny. Not only is Taylor born on 13 December, she turned 13 on Friday 13th, her first album went gold in 13 weeks and her first number-one song had a 13-second intro. "Basically whenever a 13 comes up in my life, it's a good thing," she said in a 2009 MTV interview. In a nod to her lucky number, the digits of *Lover*, *Folklore*, and *Midnights* album release dates also each add up to 13.

Image: Fred Duval / Film Magic / Getty Images

THE NUMBER 13 IS TAYLOR'S FAVOURITE — SHE WENT THROUGH A PHRASE OF DRAWING IT ONTO HER HAND

FOLKLORE

FOLKLORE

BREAKING RECORDS AT EVERY TURN, TAYLOR'S METEORIC CULTURAL IMPACT WILL LONG GO DOWN IN HISTORY

FOLKLORE

⏵ A shocked-looking Taylor picks up the award for Entertainer of the Year at the Annual Country Music Association Awards in 2009. Just 19 at the time, she was the youngest ever country star to receive the accolade, but she was breaking records way earlier than this. In 2006, after the release of 'Our Song', she became the youngest artist in history to have written and performed a number one song on the Hot Country Songs chart.

Image: Rick Diamond / Getty images

⏵ Since winning her first Grammy Award, Taylor has tallied up 12 in total and gone on to set even more records. She is the first and only woman to win thrice – that's three times – in the prestigious Album of the Year category, with Fearless (2009), 1989 (2016) and Folklore (2021), and is the female artist with the most nominations for Song of the Year, despite never winning the accolade.

Image: Jay L. Clendenin / Los Angeles Times / Getty images

⏵ Both rising to fame in the late noughties, it's no surprise Taylor became friends with Miley Cyrus – she even had a cameo in Hannah Montana: The Movie. Here the pals perform 'Fifteen' together at the 2009 Grammy Awards. Fast forward one year and Taylor scooped the Grammy for Album of the Year for Fearless, making her the youngest artist at the time to triumph in the category.

Image: Kevin Mazur / Getty images

SINCE WINNING HER FIRST GRAMMY, TAYLOR HAS TALLIED UP 12 IN TOTAL

Fun Fact

TAYLOR CAN ALSO ADD AWARD-WINNING FILMMAKER TO HER JAM-PACKED RESUME. IN 2021, SHE WROTE AND DIRECTED *ALL TOO WELL: THE SHORT FILM* – A 14-MINUTE VIDEO STARRING SADIE SINK AND DYLAN O'BRIEN AS THE YOUNG LOVERS WHOSE ILL-FATED RELATIONSHIP IS CHRONICLED IN THE LYRICS OF THE 2012 POWER BALLAD. THE SINGER-TURNED-FILMMAKER THEN SCOOPED THREE AWARDS FOR THE FILM AT THE 2022 MTV VIDEO MUSIC AWARDS, INCLUDING BEST DIRECTION, BEST LONGFORM VIDEO AND THE HIGHLY COVETED VIDEO OF THE YEAR. THIS HAS MADE TAYLOR THE FIRST ARTIST EVER TO WIN VIDEO OF THE YEAR THREE TIMES, AND THE FIRST ARTIST IN HISTORY TO WIN VIDEO OF THE YEAR FOR A SELF-DIRECTED VIDEO.

Image: Dimitrios Kambouris / Getty Images

FOLKLORE

- While Taylor can't quite match Beyonce's 32 Grammys, the 'Anti-Hero' singer has a mammoth 40 American Music Awards to her name. She dominated the 2022 ceremony, taking home all six awards she was nominated for. This haul makes her the artist with the most wins at the annual awards, easily eclipsing second-ranked Michael Jackson with his 26 trophies.

Image: Tommaso Boddi / WireImage / Getty images

- Looking glam in black sequins, Taylor performs at the Nashville Songwriters Awards in 2022, before being named the Songwriter-Artist of the Decade. Her set included 'All Too Well (10-minute version)', a song she re-recorded for *RED (Taylor's Version)* and which is now the longest single in history to reach number one in the Billboard Hot 100.

Image: Terry Wyatt / Getty images

- Walking the red carpet at the 2022 MTV Video Music Awards (VMAs), Taylor is certainly no stranger to coming out on top at this star-studded event. In 2022 alone, she picked up four awards, making her the only artist to have ever won the highly coveted video of the year award three times – for 'Bad Blood' (2015), 'You Need to Calm Down' (2019) and 'All Too Well' (2022).

Image: Arturo Holmes/FilmMagic / Getty images

FOLKLORE

IN 2022, SHE PICKED UP FOUR MTV AWARDS, MAKING HER THE ONLY ARTIST TO HAVE EVER WON THE VIDEO OF THE YEAR AWARD THREE TMES

For many, the most memorable MTV VMAs moment involving Taylor was in 2009 when Kanye West interrupted her on stage mid-acceptance speech. But she's also put on some iconic performances, like at the 2015 ceremony when she joined Nicki Minaj on stage for a mash-up of 'The Night is Still Young' and 'Bad Blood', stomping out rumours of a supposed feud between the two singers.

Image: John Shearer / Getty images

FOLKLORE

▾
The silverware in Taylor's trophy cabinet doesn't just reflect her talent as a singer-songwriter. In December 2011, she was bestowed with the Harmony Award at the Nashville Symphony Ball, which paid tribute to how she reflects the unique harmony between the many worlds of music that exist in Nashville.

Image: Royce DeGrie / Getty images

▴
At the 2019 American Music Awards, Taylor received the first ever Artist of the Decade award. To celebrate this honour, she performed a medley of her best tracks, which culminated in 'Lover' with the singer adorned in a bubble-gum pink cape. During her acceptance speech, the singer said the honour celebrated ten years of "hard work and of art and of fun and memories".

Image: Emma McIntyre/AMA2019 / Getty images

FOLKLORE

> Taylor might have left school at 17 to pursue a career in music, but in 2022 she received an honorary doctorate in fine arts from New York University. At the ceremony in the city's iconic Yankee Stadium, she gave a rousing speech to graduates advising them to follow their 'gut instincts' even in the face of fear.
>
> Image: Angela Weiss / AFP / Getty images

- Dressed in a statement bejewelled jumpsuit at the 2023 iHeartRadio Music Awards, Taylor took home the Song of the Year award for 'Anti-Hero'. The track is taken from her album *Midnights*, which made Spotify history when it was released on 1 October 2022 by becoming the most streamed album on a single day. With 184 million streams, it beat the previous record of 153 million streams set by Drake's *Certified Lover Boy*.

Image: Jeff Kravitz / Getty images

FOLKLORE

TAYLOR WAS PRESENTED WITH THE BRIT'S GLOBAL ICON AWARD IN 2021 TO RECOGNISE HER IMMENSE IMPACT ON MUSIC AROUND THE WORLD

Did you know?

WHEN TAYLOR RELEASED HER ALBUM *FOLKLORE* IN JULY 2020, IT SPARKED A MAJOR BUZZ AROUND THE TERM 'FOLKLORE'. IN RESPONSE TO A GIGANTIC INFLUX OF INTERNET USERS SEARCHING FOR THE WORD'S DEFINITION, THE AMERICAN FOLKLORE SOCIETY LAUNCHED A NEW WEBSITE TITLED 'WHAT IS FOLKLORE?', WHILE FOLKLORISTS WERE RECRUITED TO HELP PROMOTE THE ACADEMIC FIELD ON SOCIAL MEDIA. THE SINGER HERSELF WEIGHED IN ON THE DISCUSSION WITH THIS INSIGHT: "A TALE THAT BECOMES FOLKLORE IS ONE THAT IS PASSED DOWN AND WHISPERED AROUND. SOMETIMES EVEN SUNG ABOUT. THE LINES BETWEEN FANTASY AND REALITY BLUR AND BOUNDARIES BETWEEN TRUTH AND FICTION BECOME ALMOST INDISCERNIBLE."

Image: Octavio Jones / TAS23 / Getty Images

FOLKLORE

▸ Loved and adored by fans on all continents, Taylor was presented with the BRIT's Global Icon Award in 2021 to recognise her immense impact on music around the world. She is the first ever female recipient of the award, which is reserved for truly exceptional artists. Previous winners include British music legends Elton John, David Bowie and Robbie Williams.

Image: Dave J Hogan / Getty images

▸ We all know Taylor is an icon, but she has the awards to prove it. In 2019, she received the inaugural Teen Icon Award at the Teen Choice Awards dressed in a colourful Versace shorts co-ord. She has won more Teen Choice Awards than any other artist in history and used the moment in 2019 to address gender pay inequality and remind young fans that mistakes are inevitable.

Image: FOX Image Collection Getty images

FOLKLORE

> Another feat only Taylor has achieved is taking over the entire top ten of the Billboard Hot 100 chart. The never-seen-before moment happened when the singer released *Midnights*, with her single 'Anti-Hero' taking the number-one spot. Here Taylor is celebrating at the Billboard Music Awards in 2019 with Panic! At The Disco's Brendon Urie.
>
> Image: Ethan Miller / Getty images

> During her 2023 Eras Tour, Taylor performed tracks from her 2022 album *Midnights* in a glittering Oscar de la Renta t-shirt. It's definitely an unforgettable era for Taylor as she once again proved her unmatched popularity, selling more than a record-breaking six million albums in less than eight weeks. The album also became the highest-selling vinyl album of the 21st century.
>
> Image: Kevin Mazur / Getty images

Fun Fact

SWIFTIES REJOICE, YOU CAN NOW STUDY TAYLOR SWIFT AT UNIVERSITY – AND THERE'S MORE THAN ONE COURSE AVAILABLE. THE POP STAR FIRST BECAME THE SUBJECT OF AN UNDERGRADUATE COURSE IN 2022 WHEN NEW YORK UNIVERSITY'S CLIVE DAVIS INSTITUTE LAUNCHED A CLASS COVERING SWIFT'S EVOLUTION AS A CREATIVE MUSIC ENTREPRENEUR. TEXAS UNIVERSITY FOLLOWED A FEW MONTHS LATER BY OFFERING A COURSE TITLED 'THE TAYLOR SWIFT SONGBOOK' WHILE THE LATEST INSTITUTION TO GET IN ON THE ACTION IS STANFORD UNIVERSITY, WITH ITS TEN-WEEK COURSE PROMISING AN IN-DEPTH ANALYSIS OF THE SONG 'ALL TOO WELL (10-MINUTE VERSION)'. THERE'S EVEN A SUMMER SCHOOL CLASS AVAILABLE IN THE UK AT THE QUEEN MARY UNIVERSITY OF LONDON, WHICH PROMPTS STUDENTS TO EXPLORE THE QUESTION 'IS THE WORK OF TAYLOR SWIFT LITERATURE?'.

Image: Dia Dipasupil / Getty Images

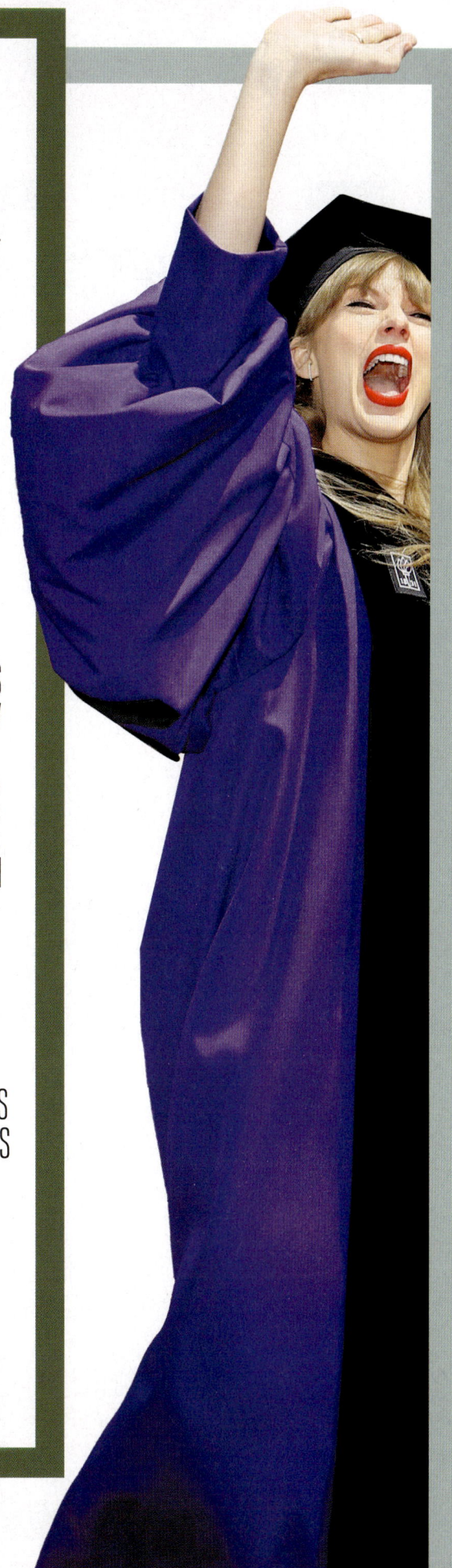

◀ The 1989 World Tour became the highest grossing tour in 2015, with critics praising the production and Taylor's mesmerising stage presence. Her performances will also be remembered for the appearances of unannounced special guests, which included a roll call of her celeb friends including the likes of Cara Delevingne, Kendall Jenner, Karlie Kloss, Martha Hunt and Gigi Hadid.

Image: Angela Weiss / Frazer Harrison / Getty images

FOLKLORE

Did you know?

TICKETS TO THE ERAS TOUR WERE IN SUCH HIGH DEMAND THE TICKETMASTER WEBSITE CRASHED ON THE FIRST DAY OF PRESALE. NEVER BEFORE HAD THE COMPANY EXPERIENCED THE SHEER FORCE OF HUNDREDS OF THOUSANDS OF SWIFTIES, AS 14 MILLION FANS SHOWED UP FOR TICKETS. EVENTUALLY TICKETMASTER HAD TO CANCEL THE PUBLIC SALE AS THERE WERE NO TICKETS LEFT. COMING UNDER MUCH CRITICISM FOR ITS FLAWED TICKETING SYSTEM, TICKETMASTER WAS EVEN SUED BY SOME CUSTOMERS WHILE LAW-MAKERS WERE SPURRED TO INVESTIGATE UNFAIR PRACTICES IN THE LIVE MUSIC PROMOTION BUSINESS. ONLY TAYLOR AND HER FANS COULD TURN A WEBSITE CRASH INTO A POLITICAL MOVEMENT.

Image: Barry King / Alamy Images

- Taylor knocked Queen of Pop Madonna off her throne in March 2023, when she performed in Glendale, Arizona, to more than 69,000 fans. This broke the 'Vogue' singer's record for the most attended female concert – she had sung to 63,000 people in 1987 at the Anaheim Stadium in Germany. Taylor has also surpassed Madonna to become the woman with the most top tens in chart history, tallying 40 top ten hits in the Hot 100 – this is two more than Madonna.

Image: Gie Knaeps / Getty images

FOLKLORE

▸ Continuing her reign as one of the most in-demand pop stars on the planet, Taylor broke world records when the Eras Tour sold over 2.4 million tickets on the first day of its presale alone. This was the most tickets sold by an artist in a single day, surpassing a record set by British singer Robbie Williams in 2005 with his Close Encounters Tour.

Image: John Medina / Getty images

▸ The reputation Stadium Tour in 2018 made Taylor the female record holder for the highest-grossing tour in the United States. Yet forecasts predict her Eras Tour will outgross this, with the US leg alone projected to generate an estimated $591 million. This means Taylor is on track to beat Madonna's record to become the highest grossing female touring artist of all time – something the 'Material Girl' singer achieved with her Sweet & Sticky tour in 2009.

Image: Don Arnold / TAS18 / Getty images

There is surely no bigger pop sensation than The Beatles, but in 2021, Taylor undid a 54-year record set by the band when she dropped *Fearless (Taylor's Version)*. It was the third number-one album the singer scored in under a year, following the release of *evermore* and *folklore*. Having three chart-topping albums within 259 days of each other, she overtook The Beatles' record of 364 days, something they achieved with the albums *Help!*, *Rubber Sole* and *Revolver*.

Image: Fox Photos / Getty images

Track four on Taylor's album *Midnights* features the melodic vocals of Lana Del Rey. Called 'Snow On The Beach', the acoustic track broke Spotify records when the album was released for the most streams in a single week for an all-female collaboration. The singers photographed here at an awards ceremony in Germany in 2012 have been friends for years, but this was their first duet.

Image: Kevin Mazur / WireImage / Getty images

FRIENDLY COMPETITION BETWEEN THE CITIES SHE TOURED TO RESULTED IN CREATIVE WAYS TO HONOUR THE SINGER

Fun Fact

THE ERAS TOUR HAS ALSO PROVEN THE HUGE IMPACT TAYLOR CAN HAVE ON THE PLACES SHE VISITS. FRIENDLY COMPETITION BETWEEN THE CITIES SHE TOURED TO RESULTED IN EVER-MORE CREATIVE WAYS TO HONOUR THE SINGER. IT BEGAN WITH GLENDALE, WHICH TEMPORARILY CHANGED ITS NAME TO SWIFT CITY WHEN IT HOSTED THE FIRST TWO SHOWS OF THE TOUR. THEN ARLINGTON IN TEXAS RENAMED THE STREET OUTSIDE THE STADIUM TO TAYLOR SWIFT WAY FOR 24 HOURS TO CELEBRATE THE SINGER'S PERFORMANCE THERE, WHILE TAMPA IN FLORIDA INVITED TAYLOR TO BECOME AN HONORARY MAYOR FOR THE DAY AND NRG STADIUM IN TEXAS WAS TEMPORARILY RENAMED 'NRG STADIUM (TAYLOR'S VERSION)'.

Image: John Medina / Getty Images

… EVERMORE

EVERMORE

FASHION ICON, FILMMAKER AND FORCE FOR GOOD: TAYLOR WILL BE REMEMBERED FOR MORE THAN JUST HER MUSIC

EVERMORE

JUST AS TAYLOR'S MUSIC EVOLVES WITH EVERY NEW ALBUM, SO DOES HER STYLE

EVERMORE

> For the *Fearless* section of the Eras setlist, Taylor channelled her second studio album by stepping out in a re-imagination of her iconic glittered fringe dress, complete with a rhinestone guitar. The outfit is part of a Swarovski crystal-embellished capsule collection designed by luxe Italian fashion brand, Roberto Cavalli.
>
> Image: Kevin Winter / Getty images

> Just as Taylor's music evolves with every new album, so does her style. This was proved during the Eras Tour when her outfits changed multiple times throughout the set to reflect each of her ten musical eras. Here she performs the acoustic section on the opening night wearing a ruffled Jessica Jones gown, reminiscent of her early days of curls, cowboy boots and flowing dresses.
>
> Image: Kevin Mazur / Getty images

EVERMORE

With 'We are never getting back together like ever' emblazoned across her Ashish t-shirt, there's no doubt Taylor is celebrating her *RED* album. The slogan changed most tour dates, but the fedora hat always stayed the same – a throwback to the preppy look of stripes, varsity jackets and short shorts she worked back on The RED Tour in 2013.

Image: Omar Vega / TAS23 / Getty images

TAYLOR CHANNELLED HER SECOND ALBUM WITH A RE-IMAGINATION OF HER GLITTERED FRINGE DRESS, COMPLETE WITH A RHINESTONE GUITAR

Capturing the fairy-tale romance of her third album, *Speak Now*, Taylor stepped out to perform 'Enchanted' to a Tampa, Florida crowd wearing a beautiful Elie Saab haute couture gown with floral tulle detailing. It can be considered a more grown-up version of the now-iconic gold Valentino dress she wore during the Speak Now Tour back in 2012.

Image: Octavio Jones / TAS23 / Getty images

Did you know?

WHEN AN 18-YEAR-OLD BILLIE EILISH WON ALBUM OF THE YEAR FOR *WHEN WE ALL FALL ASLEEP, WHERE DO WE GO?* AT THE 2020 GRAMMY AWARDS, SHE BROKE TAYLOR'S RECORD FOR BEING THE YOUNGEST EVER ARTIST TO TAKE HOME THE HIGHLY COVETED AWARD. BUT THERE IS A LOT OF LOVE BETWEEN THE TWO STARS, WITH BILLIE FANGIRLING OVER OLD-SCHOOL TAYLOR SONGS AND ACKNOWLEDGING HOW THE OLDER SINGER'S EFFORTS TO CALL OUT MALE PRIVILEGE IN THE MUSIC INDUSTRY HAS POSITIVELY IMPACTED HER OWN JOURNEY IN THE BUSINESS. TAYLOR RETURNED THE ADORATION BY SAYING BILLIE WAS ONE OF THE MOST INFLUENTIAL FEMALE POP ARTISTS.

Image: Kevin Mazur / Getty Images

Taylor opened The Eras Tour each night wearing different variations of a rainbow-hued Atelier Versace bodysuit, referencing the dreamy pastel aesthetic of her *Lover* album. To perform 'The Man', she pulled on this sequined pinstripe Versace blazer over the top for a fiercer vibe befitting of the feminist anthem.

Image: Octavio Jones / TAS23 / Getty images

EVERMORE

The most dramatic look of The Eras Tour was easily Roberto Cavalli's one-legged jumpsuit. The design featured a three-dimensional, embroidered snake motif winding from Taylor's ankle to the top of her leg, leaving nobody guessing she was in *reputation* era mode. While touring this album in 2018, the set featured a huge python in response to Kim Kardashian's online name calling.

Image: Terence Rushin / TAS23 / Getty images

WHILE TOURING IN 2018, THE SET FEATURED A HUGE PYTHON IN RESPONSE TO KIM KARDASHIAN'S ONLINE NAME CALLING

Taylor celebrated her *1989* album by singing the likes of 'Shake It Off' and 'Bad Blood' wearing another glittering Roberto Cavalli outfit – this time a two piece co-ord spotted in red, orange and green depending on the tour date. The costume paid tribute to the sequin-clad outfits that defined The 1989 World Tour in 2015.

Image: Kevin Winter / Getty images

EVERMORE

⊙ Lace, plaid and a red lip will forever be associated with Taylor's *evermore* album and she brought the cottage core styling to the stage by wearing a whimsical orange prairie dress complete with a ruffled, embroidered bodice. Referencing the nature imagery present throughout the 15 album tracks, she even performed on a moss-covered piano.

Image: Kevin Winter / Getty images

⊙ Rounding off the three-hour-long setlist with tracks from *Midnights*, Taylor closed the show on opening night wearing this midnight blue leotard designed by Oscar de la Renta. The aesthetic of the 2022 album is heavily 1970s-influenced, from the autumnal palette of the record's artwork to shimmering disco pizazz, as exemplified by this retro-glam outfit.

Image: Kevin Mazur / Getty images

⊙ Wearing a delicate chiffon Alberta Ferretti gown, Taylor was in full folksy mode when singing her ethereal melodies from *folklore*. The cosy cabin in the woods she dreamt up while writing the album in lockdown made it into the set, reminding us of how she managed to propel the prairie aesthetic into peak popularity.

Image: Ethan Miller / TAS23 / Getty images

THE COSY CABIN IN THE WOODS SHE DREAMT UP WHILE WRITING THE ALBUM IN LOCKDOWN MADE IT INTO THE SET

102

EVERMORE

○ On another performance of 'The Man', Taylor strutted her stuff in this silver-clad Versace blazer. The song marked a pivotal point for the singer when it was released, as it was the first track she solo directed a music video for. She has since directed the music videos for 'Cardigan', 'Willow', 'Anti-Hero', 'Bejewelled' as well as 'Lavender Haze'.

Image: John Medina / Stringer / Getty images

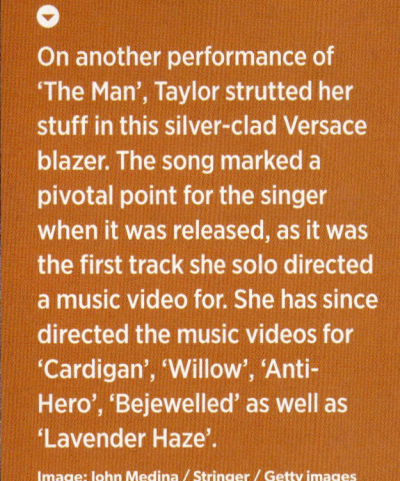

○ From directing music videos to making her own short films, Taylor is certainly expanding her skillset and picking up awards in the process. *All Too Well: A Short Film* racked up an American Music Award, a Grammy and a Hollywood Critics Award. She also brought a whole new level of publicity to the Toronto International Film Festival, where Swifties camped out overnight to catch a glimpse of the singer on the red carpet ahead of a screening of the film.

Image: VALERIE MACON /AFP / Getty images

EVERMORE

○ Proving herself to be a creative powerhouse, Taylor was also the subject of *Miss Americana*, a 2020 documentary film following the singer over the course of several years. It takes place during a transitional phase of her career as she wraps up the 2018 Reputation Stadium Tour and begins creating her album, *Lover*. This still from the Netflix documentary shows the star backstage, prepping for her appearance on the 2019 MTV Video Music Awards.

Image: Ron Harvey / Getty images

▶ Dressed in a Carmen March houndstooth jumpsuit, Taylor attends the *Miss Americana* premiere at the 2020 Sundance Film Festival. Critics have praised the documentary for the 'emotional heft' of Taylor's interviews, which discussed issues including eating disorders, self-esteem and sexual assault. There was an unprecedented surge in attendees at the festival and increased media coverage thanks to Taylor's presence.

Image: Neilson Barnard / Getty images

EVERMORE

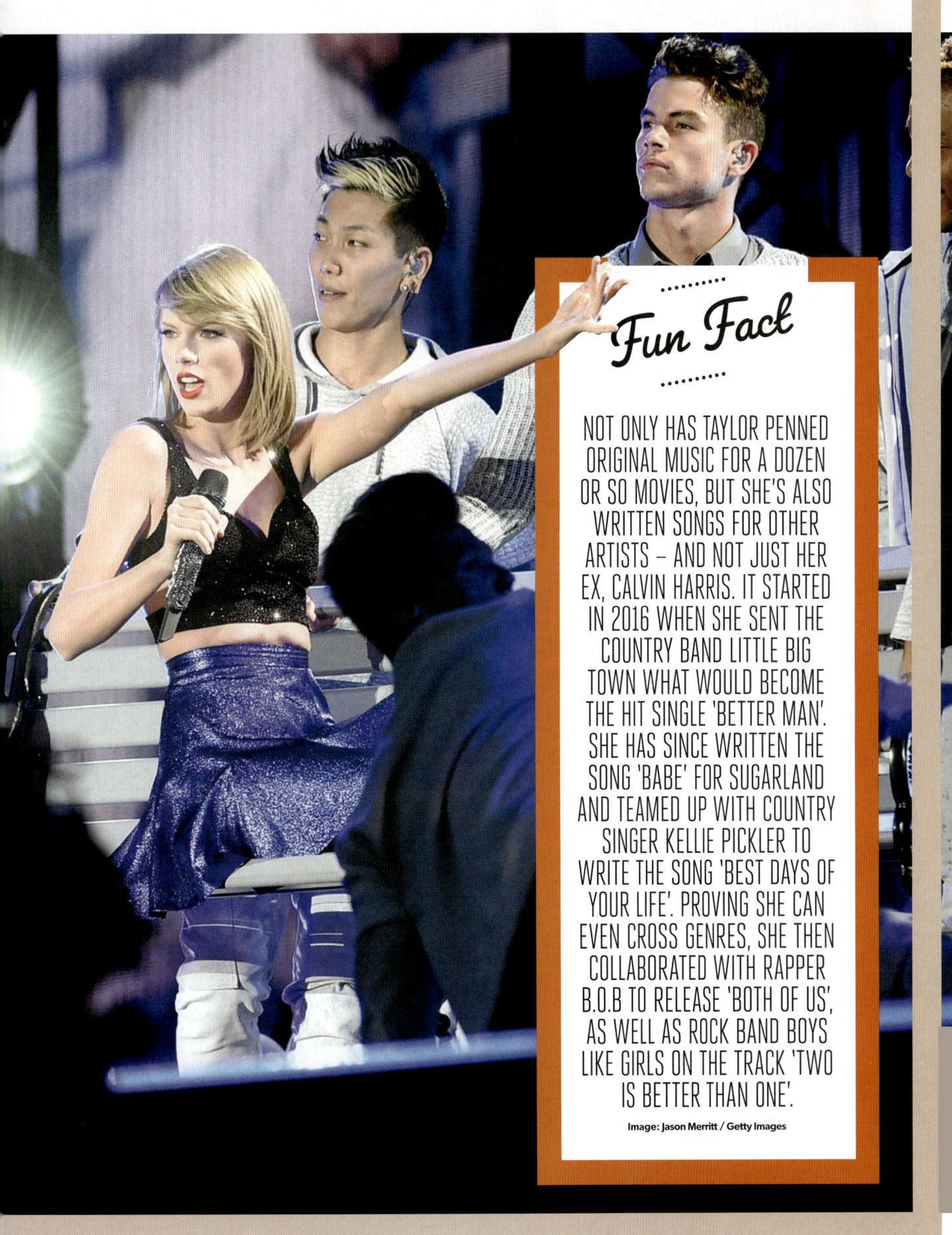

Fun Fact

NOT ONLY HAS TAYLOR PENNED ORIGINAL MUSIC FOR A DOZEN OR SO MOVIES, BUT SHE'S ALSO WRITTEN SONGS FOR OTHER ARTISTS – AND NOT JUST HER EX, CALVIN HARRIS. IT STARTED IN 2016 WHEN SHE SENT THE COUNTRY BAND LITTLE BIG TOWN WHAT WOULD BECOME THE HIT SINGLE 'BETTER MAN'. SHE HAS SINCE WRITTEN THE SONG 'BABE' FOR SUGARLAND AND TEAMED UP WITH COUNTRY SINGER KELLIE PICKLER TO WRITE THE SONG 'BEST DAYS OF YOUR LIFE'. PROVING SHE CAN EVEN CROSS GENRES, SHE THEN COLLABORATED WITH RAPPER B.O.B TO RELEASE 'BOTH OF US', AS WELL AS ROCK BAND BOYS LIKE GIRLS ON THE TRACK 'TWO IS BETTER THAN ONE'.

Image: Jason Merritt / Getty Images

Did you know?

TAYLOR IS AS MUCH A FORCE ON TIKTOK AS SHE IS IN MUSIC. HER UBER-LOYAL FANS HAVE BEEN CULTIVATING A FEVERED COLLECTIVE ON THE PLATFORM KNOWN AS SWIFTTOK, WHERE THEY GO TO RANK HER SONGS, REVIEW HER ALBUMS AND SHOW OFF THEIR VINYL. IN FACT, THE ONLINE COMMUNITY DISSECTS EVERY MOVE THE SINGER MAKES WITH LABORATORY PRECISION. FROM MERCH RELEASES AND RED CARPET APPEARANCES, TO SOCIAL MEDIA POSTS AND MUSIC VIDEOS – NO ACTION IS IGNORED AS SWIFTIES CLAMBER TO PREDICT TAYLOR'S NEXT STEPS. THIS IS JUST ANOTHER EXAMPLE OF HOW TAYLOR'S FANBASE IS AMONG THE MOST DEVOTED IN THE WORLD.

Image: Jun Sato / TAS18 / Getty Images

Taylor wrote and directed a documentary concert film called *folklore: The Long Pond Studio Sessions*, available to watch on Disney Plus. In the programme, Taylor performs all 17 tracks of her eighth album, *folklore*, while discussing the creative process and inspiration behind the songs with her co-producers Aaron Dessner and Jack Antonoff.

Image: Everett Collection / Alamy images

EVERMORE

After a small role in dystopian sci-fi movie *The Giver*, Taylor took a five-year acting hiatus before returning to filmdom in 2019 as Bombalurina in *Cats* – the movie adaption of Andrew Lloyd Webber's stage musical of the same name. Starring alongside big names including Jennifer Hudson, Judi Dench, James Corden and Rebel Wilson, she penned an original number for the film called 'Beautiful Ghosts' which went on to receive a Grammy nomination.

Image: Taylor Hill / FilmMagic / Getty images

The pop star is no stranger to the silver screen either. In 2012, she voiced the character Audrey in Dr Seuss' *The Lorax* – the CGI animated film starring Zac Efron and Danny DeVito. But it was not her first acting role. A big *CSI* fan, she had played a rebellious teenager in one episode of the crime drama in 2009 and made her feature film debut in 2010 in the romcom *Valentine's Day*.

Image: Kevin Winter / Getty images

EVERMORE

TAYLOR SWIFT

🔽 Whether it's standing up to industry bullies or fighting for ownership of her own songs, Taylor has long been paving the way for women in the music industry. Among the younger generation of female artists who cite the singer-songwriter as an inspiration are Olivia Rodrigo, Maisie Peters, Phoebe Bridgers and Gayle, seen here opening for Taylor on The Eras Tour.

Image: Omar Vega / TAS23 / Getty images

FROM THE DIRECTOR OF AMERICAN HUSTLE AND SILVER LININGS PLAYBOOK

AMSTERDAM
LET THE LOVE, MURDER AND CONSPIRACY BEGIN.

🔼 More recently you might have spotted Taylor on the promotional posters for the 1930s-set mystery thriller, *Amsterdam*. Playing the character Elizabeth Meekins, she shares the credits of the 2022 film with a long list of Hollywood stalwarts such as Margot Robbie, Christian Bale, Anya Taylor-Joy, Rami Malek and Robert De Niro.

Image: Everett Collection / Alamy images

EVERMORE

Fun Fact

TAYLOR'S MOVIE-MAKING SKILLS WILL BE COMING TO THE BIG SCREEN SOON, COURTESY OF AMERICAN STUDIO SEARCHLIGHT PICTURES. ALTHOUGH MANY DETAILS ABOUT TAYLOR'S FEATURE-LENGTH DIRECTIONAL DEBUT ARE BEING KEPT UNDER WRAPS, WE KNOW SHE HAS PENNED THE SCRIPT. "I'D LOVE TO KEEP TAKING BABY STEPS FORWARD," SHE SAID DURING A DISCUSSION AT THE 2022 TORONTO FILM FESTIVAL. "AND I THINK THAT I'M AT A PLACE NOW WHERE THE NEXT BABY STEP IS NOT A BABY STEP. IT WOULD BE COMMITTING TO MAKING A FILM. AND I FEEL LIKE I WOULD JUST ABSOLUTELY LOVE FOR THE RIGHT OPPORTUNITY TO ARISE BECAUSE I JUST ABSOLUTELY, ABSOLUTELY ADORE TELLING STORIES THIS WAY."

Image: Bob Levey / TAS23 / Getty Images

Taylor is not just making an impact on upcoming names in the music industry. She is also behind what guitar manufacturer Fender terms the 'Taylor Swift factor' – the phenomenon of rising guitar sales among women. Originally thought to be a short-term spike, the singer's influence was underestimated, as females continue to drive sales and actually make up half of those who are learning to play the instrument.

Image: Octavio Jones / TAS23 / Getty images

109

Did you know?

IT'S ALREADY COMMON KNOWLEDGE THAT TAYLOR WROTE THE ORIGINAL SONG 'CAROLINA' FOR THE 2022 FILM ADAPTATION OF *WHERE THE CRAWDADS SING*. BUT FEW REALISE THE IDEA WAS ENTIRELY THE SINGER'S OWN. AFTER FALLING IN LOVE WITH THE BOOK BY DELIA OWENS A FEW YEARS AGO, SHE PENNED THE NEW PIECE OF MUSIC AS SOON SHE HEARD REESE WITHERSPOON WAS PRODUCING THE MOVIE VERSION AND IT WAS GOING TO STAR BRITISH ACTRESS DAISY EDGAR-JONES. "I WANTED TO CREATE SOMETHING HAUNTING AND ETHEREAL TO MATCH THIS MESMERISING STORY," SWIFT SAID. LUCKILY REESE AND HER TEAM WERE OVERJOYED, SAYING THEY WERE "THE BENEVOLENT RECEIVERS OF [AN] INCREDIBLE ARTISTIC GIFT".

Image: Album / Alamy Images

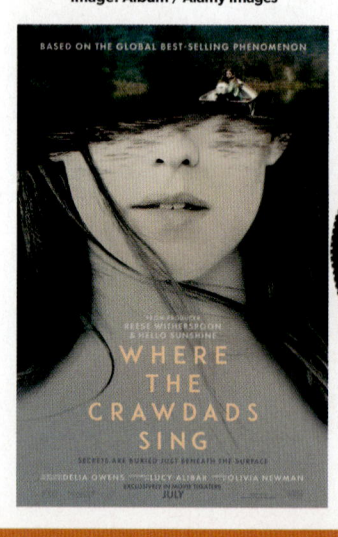

In the midst of re-recording her first six albums, Taylor is gradually reclaiming control over the music she has created and single-handedly reshaping the way wealth is distributed in the industry. By upending the system, she is paving the way for other artists to do the same and proving herself to be an invaluable change-marker along the way.

Image: Bob Levey / TAS23 / Getty images

EVERMORE

As well as being one of the best song-writers and performers on the planet, Taylor's marketing game is also up there with the best. From writing intimate blogs on Myspace and Tumblr, to breadcrumbing her Twitter and Instagram followers ahead of album releases, she has used social media to stay connected to her fans in a way no other pop star has been able to replicate.

Image: PjrStudio / Alamy images

A perfect example of Taylor's marketing genius is how she kept fans hooked in the lead-up to the release of *Midnights*. After taking to Instagram Live to describe the forthcoming record, she posted a series of videos on TikTok titled 'Midnights mayhem with me' where she used a bingo cage to randomly select one song off the 13-track album and announce its title. She also worked with Spotify to release lyric snippets on billboards around the world, catering to all her global fanbase.

Image: Hazel Plater / Alamy images

SHE HAS USED SOCIAL MEDIA TO STAY CONNECTED TO HER FANS IN A WAY NO OTHER POP STAR HAS BEEN ABLE TO

111

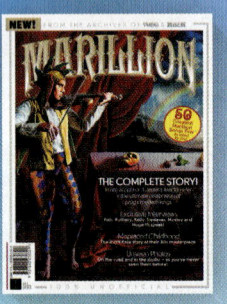

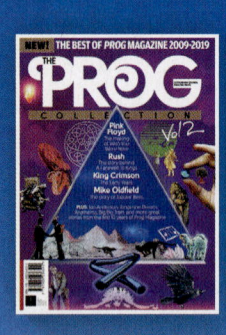

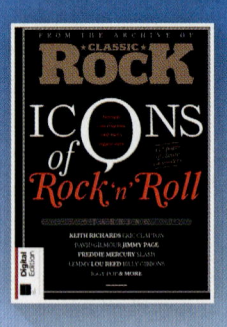

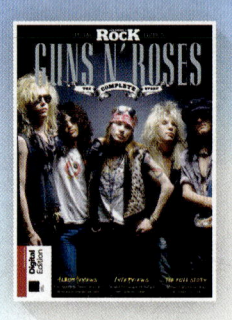

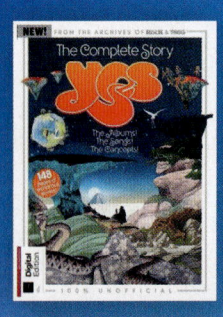

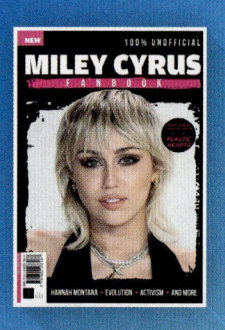

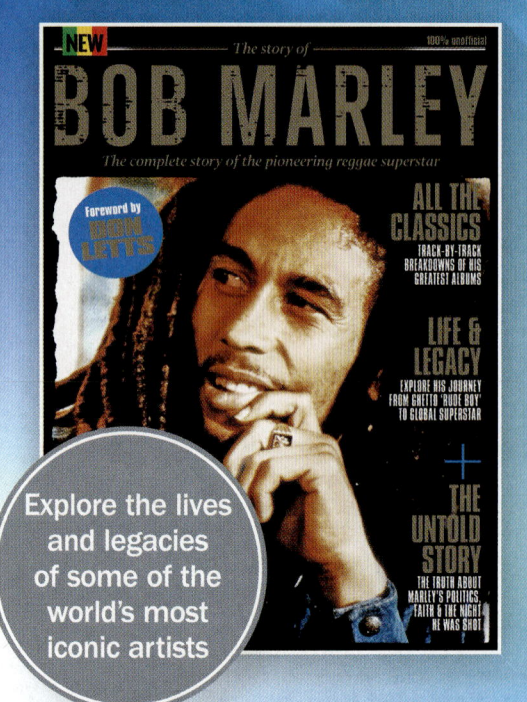

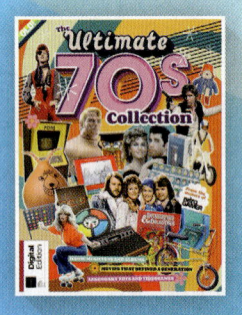

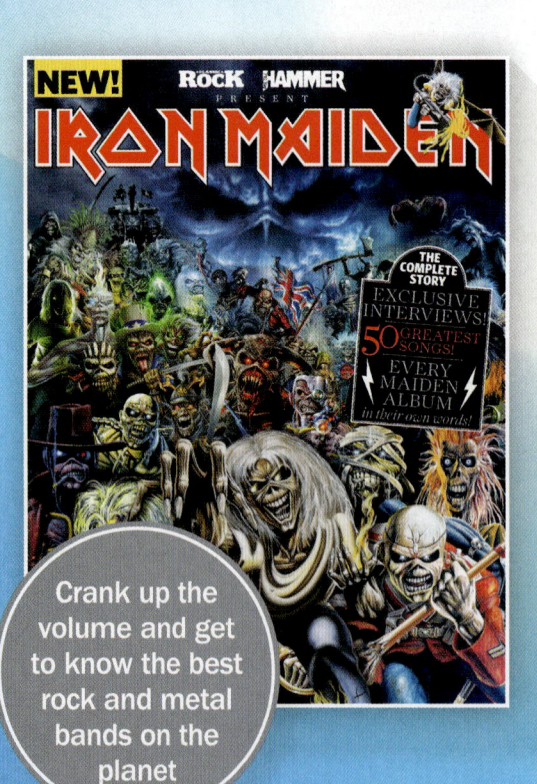

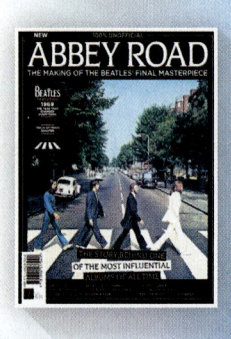

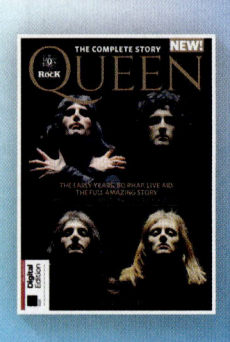

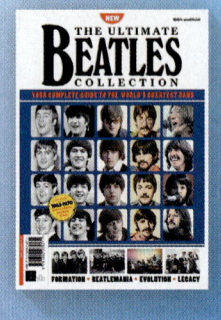

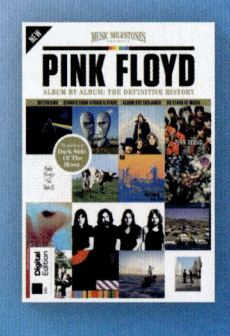

Celebrate the songs and sounds of the greatest decades in music

Explore the lives and legacies of some of the world's most iconic artists

Crank up the volume and get to know the best rock and metal bands on the planet

✓ Get great savings when you buy direct from us

✓ 1000s of great titles, many not available anywhere else

✓ World-wide delivery and super-safe ordering

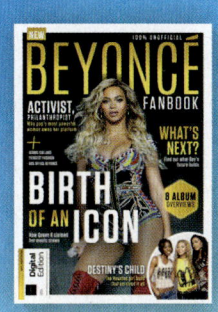

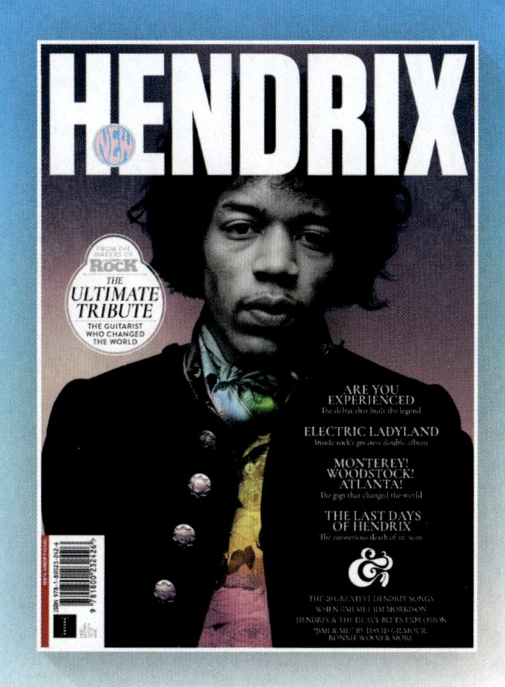

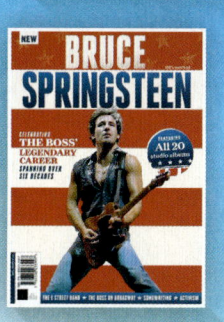

ROCK ON WITH OUR MUSIC BOOKAZINES

Discover the origins of legendary songs, relive iconic performances and meet the pioneers behind some of music's greatest names

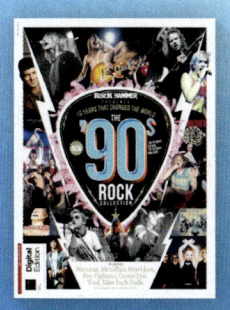

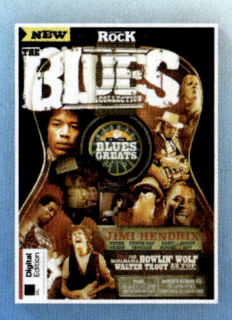

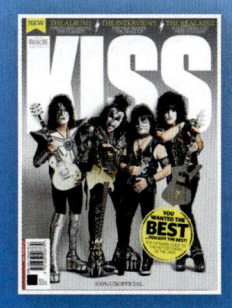

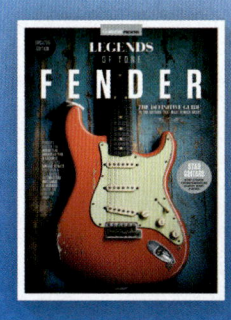

Discover everything there is to know about your favourite pop stars

Follow us on Instagram @futurebookazines

www.magazinesdirect.com
Magazines, back issues & bookazines.

SUBSCRIBE & SAVE UP TO 61%

Delivered direct to your door or straight to your device

Choose from over 80 magazines and make great savings off the store price!

Binders, books and back issues also available

Simply visit www.magazinesdirect.com

✓ No hidden costs 🚚 Shipping included in all prices 🌐 We deliver to over 100 countries 🔒 Secure online payment

FUTURE **magazinesdirect.com**
Official Magazine Subscription Store